Advance praise for **Breakthrough**

"If you want to be an exceptional communicator, you must read Bill's book."

—Robert Thompson, CEO, Quality Ingredients Corporation

"Breakthrough is a guided examination of the thinking that keeps us forever doing what we have always done. Through his experiences as a consultant, father and husband, Bill models and provides easy to follow exercises to create the "Breakthrough" mindset that has a positive impact on work and life. If you've been battle-scarred and disillusioned from previous attempts to achieve your goals I encourage you to read the last chapter first. Every prior chapter focuses you on exactly what you need to know to create Breakthrough. I plan to use Bill's framework in consulting with all of my clients."

—C. Dan McArthur, Author of Outcome Management,
Managing Director, CapSources, Inc.

"Very few people understand the powerful competitive advantage derived from a group of people effectively working together. Even fewer understand that to maximize this process, there must be a culture of mutual respect practiced. Bill Mills understands this culture and is able to communicate these values and the process."

—Bob Cervenka, Founder & Chairman of the Board, Phillips
Plastics Corporation

"Breakthrough is an entertaining and valuable read. It is a practical guide to creating better outcomes in your personal and professional life by managing your feelings, the basis for many actions, through the power of healthy self-talk."

—*Grant McLennan, former Chairman and CEO of SmarteCarte*

"Bill Mills has presented a common sense approach to introspection. Clearly, how we think affects everything we do and experience. We all need help staying in touch with what we are thinking and learning to be sure we don't let these thoughts drive thoughtless or unproductive behavior. The idea of Conscious Conversation with yourself is a very useful technique for making this happen."

—*Wallace Stettinius, retired Chairman and CEO of Cadmus Communications, currently Senior Executive Fellow at VCU School of Business*

"Bill has placed communication and relationship building exactly where it belongs, on our personal shoulders. He writes using life experiences that each of us can relate to because we've all been in similar situations. Readers will certainly be better prepared to achieve life success after reading and applying the principles outlined in this book."

—*Bill Schult, President, Maximum Potential, Inc.*

"Having worked with Bill Mills and his ideas for nearly 10 years, I have seen literally hundreds of people benefit from these principles. Read and apply these great thoughts and you, too, will experience a BREAK-THROUGH in your life!"

—*Rich Meiss, President, Meiss Education Institute*

"Bill teaches how to design your life in a manner that results in breakthrough achievements. And he does it using practical, authentic life stories. You will find his ideas to be immediately applicable to your business, your marriage and your life."

—*Eric Jackson, President, Phoenix Packaging Corporation*

"Bill's book is both exhilarating and freeing. His "WWIINN" strategy will produce immediate results. Your life will be revitalized! Enjoy!"

—*Bernie Borschke, Director of Human Resources, AmeriPride*

"Breakthrough is a fascinating read. I would highly recommend this book as mandatory reading for anyone that interacts with or manages people on a daily basis. The issues uncovered in Breakthrough are the real daily interactive issues we all have to deal with."

—*William Klocke, Vice President / General Manager, Southern Graphic Systems*

Breakthrough

The Power of Conscious Conversation

Breakthrough

The Power of
Conscious Conversation
5 Laws for Getting
What You Want
from Life

William Stewart Mills

Beaver's Pond Press, Inc.
Edina, Minnesota

ISBN 1-931646-92-9

Library of Congress Catalog Number: 2002115487

Printed in the United States of America

First Printing: February 2003

06 05 04 03   6 5 4 3 2 1

Beaver's Pond Press, Inc.   7104 Ohms Lane Suite 216
                                         Edina, MN 55439-1465
                                         (952) 829-8818
                                         www.beaverspondpress.com

to order, visit *www.bookhousefulfillment.com* or call 1-800-752-3303. Reseller discounts available.

Table of Contents

Foreword

Why is there no such thing as idle conversation? In this challenging book, you will meet a remarkable author who will reveal a pathway to achieving what you want and deserve. I met William Mills several years ago on the client end of a business-consulting project. As a consultant, I know that Bill delivers insight and translates that insight into value. Although he is as scientific and thoughtful as anyone, his work is unique because it is also practical and useful. My special appreciation for Bill's work is directly related to his experience in the real world laboratory where life and work happen, not just a theoretical platform that tells you what to do but not how to do it. Bill will help you connect important distinctions about the value of conversations and their ability to create real success and fulfillment.

I've watched Bill give lectures and always noted his extraordinary connection with the audience. His experience as a misplaced civil engineer and his commitment to voracious reading as he struggled to achieve served him well. Now, as a consultant, he has something figured out . . . the breakthrough we all desire, the power that few people have found, isn't so illusive after all.

I love how this book is presented with rich experiences derived from success, failure, love, marriage—the entire range of human experience and its relevance to our search for the skills that allow us to harness conversations to serve our life's purpose.

I say, "Salute to Bill Mills and his wife Lisa for sharing the toolbox we all need to transform our conversations to personal achievement and satisfaction."

—Paul Horgen, CEO IBM MidAmerica Credit Union

Introduction

I believe in people. People fascinate, frustrate, encourage and inspire me. And for the longest time people baffled me. Why do they do what they do? Why do they spend so much time in conflict and pain? Why are some apparently happy and successful while others seem trapped in unfulfilling jobs and relationships?

In my 20s and 30s I was a sponge for any information that would help me become more successful. My car was a wasteland of audiocassettes on philosophy, human psychology, selling strategies, personal mastery and time management. I unlocked the giant within. I felt the fear and did it anyway. I reprogrammed myself and followed my bliss. I read my affirmations and visualized my future while I dressed for success.

And I set goals. Lots of them. Goals to lose weight (gained it back). Goals to re-ignite my marriage (got divorced). And goals to be a millionaire by age 40 (at 40 I was worth about $40,000). I found that goal-setting as conventionally taught is a flawed system and that when you overstrategize, overprioritize and overcompartmentalize your life you just may miss what you're looking for when it comes.

Life, love and business are fundamentally simple. We make them difficult when we get caught up in the illusions society offers. This book describes the ideas and beliefs that have been most useful to my clients and me. Their power lies in their elegance.

As you read this book you'll become more sensitized to the many stories that are whispered in your ear or thrown in your face. You'll begin to see how these stories affect the way people operate and you'll become keenly aware of what you can do to author your life in a way that gives you more happiness, love and success.

It is the simple power of conscious conversation.

Chapter One
Behavior is Conversation

Adam and Eve have some serious explaining to do.

As I understand it, the plan was for men and women to live happily ever after in a beautiful garden in constant communion with God. There was no government, no taxation, and no laws. I think it must have been something like Club Med without the alcohol.

The closest thing to a law was God's request that no one eat any apples. (In legal terms the apple tree would be called an attractive nuisance.)

The specifics about the actual conversations between Adam and Eve are quite sketchy. However, one could imagine the following exchange:

> **Adam:** What's for dinner tonight?
>
> **Eve:** Bananas.
>
> **Adam:** That's it?
>
> **Eve:** Unless you want to try some apples.
>
> **Adam:** Hmmm.

And that's how it works. The first law of conscious conversation: human behavior is a perfect reflection of the conversation that created it. Behavior is conversation in action.

This afternoon I had a minor difference of opinion with my wife, Lisa. Lisa is a woman of passion and conviction. She is almost always right. I also like to be right. As I turned away from her I held the following conversation in my head: "Why is she so stubborn? Why can't she be tolerant of other people, like I am? Just because we disagree doesn't mean I'm stupid. How dare she think I'm stupid! I'm smart!"

By the time I'd turned around, I heard myself sigh out loud. I noticed my jaw tighten, and my temperature climbed a degree or two. All these reactions were perfectly related to the conversation I was having with myself.

Then I had a different conversation with myself. "A heavy sigh is how you express defeat. There is no defeat here. Don't take this personally. Her feelings are hers, let her have them. Wow, look how well you're handling this!"

This conversation produced a small smile and my whole body felt a bit lighter. Total elapsed time for both conversations: about three seconds.

The conversations we have with ourselves and others are based on how we interpret life. That interpretation instantly creates a flood of neuropeptides, which wash through our entire body in an instant. Do we perceive an angry face and a raised voice as a threat to our safety? If so, the peptides quickly stimulate a release of adrenaline to equip us for a fight (or in my case a three-minute mile).

What happens if we interpret a smile and kind words to mean we are safe and loved? Then the peptide wash stimulates the release of chemicals that improve our immune system. Endorphins (the natural equivalent to morphine) course through our body and we feel free and happy, but with none of morphine's side effects.

When someone behaves in a way that irritates you, you have a real opportunity to examine yourself. What conversation do you hold in your head? Is the transgressor a jerk who didn't follow your directions? After all, your directions should always be followed to the letter, shouldn't they? Your way is the only right way, isn't it? People should see life the way you see it and adhere to your values, right?

> *"The level of thinking that created the problem will not be sufficient to resolve it."*
> *—Einstein*

Each conversation creates a specific and quantifiable outcome right down to the molecules created in your body. If you want different outcomes, you need new conversations.

I have found that I am happy almost all the time. I love my wife with an intensity I didn't know was possible. I have feelings of gratitude and appreciation that seem to bubble up so often that I just have to tell the people who inspired them how important they are to me. I regularly experience contentment, satisfaction, love, excitement, and accomplishment even though I'm not a millionaire and I still want to lose a few pounds. I can trace all of these outcomes to the conversations I have with others and myself.

In the rest of this book I'll share with you the information you'll need to design your life with your words. I don't guarantee you'll become fabulously wealthy or that you'll never be subjected to hardships or pain.

What I do promise is this. If you internalize the concepts and techniques in this book you will be able to eliminate the source of 95% of your unhappiness. With practice, you will experience deeper, more fulfilling relationships, and you'll improve your ability to stand up for yourself and others.

And if you do happen to make a few million along the way, I say we split it.

The First Law of Conscious Conversation

Behavior is a perfect reflection of the conversation that created it.

Which unconcious conversations might explain my most common irritations? (For example, the internal conversation that "people should agree with me" could explain why some people are so annoying.)

_____

_____

_____

_____

How is my treatment of others a reflection of my unconcious conversations? (For example, do I sulk or bully people when we disagree?)

_____

_____

_____

_____

Chapter Two
Cutting through the B.S.[1]

A young apprentice asks the wise philosopher to take him under his wing and educate him in the ways of higher thought. The old sage agrees on one condition. "First," he says, "tell me what you know." "Lots of things," answers the novice as his chest swells slightly. "I know how to build a tent, I know right from wrong, I . . ."

Raising his hand the old man stops the boy in mid sentence. "I'm sorry," he says. "I don't think this is going to work out."

"Please," begs the young man, "give me another chance. I'll think about it all night and I'll have an answer by morning." "Very well," says the old sage.

The next day the apprentice returns and proudly states, "There is one thing I know, sir. I know that I am alive." The old philosopher shakes his head, "I'm sorry, but I cannot work with you."

"Wait!" cries the young man. "Just give me one more chance!" Three days go by and the philosopher looks up

---

1 Belief System

to see the young man slowly making his way up the path. "Master," he says, barely holding back his tears, "I can't become your apprentice."

"And why is that?" whispers the sage,

"I've realized I don't actually *know* anything."

"Very good," replies the old man with the hint of a smile. "Now we can get started."

Each of us lives in a reality of his or her own making. We take the information from our five senses, filter it through our belief system, and what's left is what we call reality. It would be more accurate to call it our personal reality. We think we know things, when in truth we interpret things.

If I am aware of a knock on the door it becomes a part of my reality. If I am aware that my conversation or actions are triggering feelings of anxiety in you, that awareness is also part of my reality. My personal reality is limited because my awareness is limited.

Dogs hear and smell things that we cannot, while birds easily see things that we are blind to. These animals experience a different reality than we do. Humans have different equipment for interpreting the world. My father is colorblind. One look at his art collection will tell you this man lives in a different world.

In addition to differences and limitations in our sensory equipment, our brain affects what we perceive as reality, and in doing so it plays a funny trick on us. It filters the available information and selects only a tiny percentage to bring to our conscious awareness. According to researchers, in the time it takes the brain to fire 10,000 synaptic relays, it presents only three to nine bits of information for our conscious awareness. This suggests we are able to access only a fraction of the information our brain is processing.

Breakthrough Opportunity

"The light which puts out our eyes is dark-ness to us. Only that day dawns to which we are awake. There is more day to dawn."
—*Henry Thoreau*

What have I decided I "know" about my boss, co-workers, family, or friends that blinds me to peace, love and happiness? (For example, if I know my spouse is insensitive, do I routinely experience anger?)

_____

_____

_____

What positive qualities might appear in my rela-tionships if I could be awake to them? (If I wasn't blinded by a person's insensitivity could I see their creativity, or courage?)

_____

_____

_____

We would likely go batty if we were conscious of hundreds or thousands of times more stimuli than we process now. So as a protection device, the brain routinely presents only the information it thinks we want.

Based upon our unique life experiences and the beliefs we have created as we've grown up, each of us has established a different filter. When a person from a Western culture meets a person from an Eastern culture, there are numerous ways they can offend each other accidentally simply because of their different beliefs about appropriate social interaction. But the emotion of being offended exists only because each person's belief system is interpreting the other's as a threat!

John Gray[2] has made a livelihood of explaining the differences between men and women using the analogy that we come from different planets. (I still haven't figured out how an entire planet came to be populated by only one gender, but then I'm not a psychologist.) His point is that other people are not you, and they do things for their reasons, not yours. That's because we filter the present through our past.

In my workshops I illustrate this point with an exercise I learned from Dr. Michael Ryce. I ask everyone to take their right hand and touch their right ear. Everyone is able to carry out the directions. Then I ask them why they put their right hand on their right ear. The most common response is, "Because you told us to." And within the limitations of our English language they are correct. However, from a scientific perspective, here is the reason they put their right hand on their right ear.

---

2 Author of *Men Are From Mars, Women Are From Venus*

1. By pushing air over my vocal chords and moving my mouth and tongue I created a series of vibrations (not sounds).

2. These vibrations traveled invisibly and undetected throughout the room until they came in contact with the ears of each person.

3. Each person's ear (antenna) picked up the vibration in the eardrum, which stimulated a psychological response inside the brain called sound.[3]

4. The brain immediately started digging through its database (memory) in an attempt to determine if these sounds had any specific meaning.

5. Because the brain had an awareness of the English language, each person knew the meaning of right, hand, ear, etc.

6. Once the message was decoded and interpreted each person acted appropriately.

7. Therefore, the reason each person was able to follow the instructions is because they shared a common history of the words. The words created a common reality and they were able to understand my request.

In our society there is a high degree of agreement around words like "right", "left" and "hand." In some form or another, we all had the common experience of learning and identifying our body parts. Someone

---

3 Scientists insist the world is devoid of color, sound, tastes and smells, but it does contain light waves, vibrations and molecules, which are translated as colors, sounds, tastes and smells inside our minds. If a tree falls in the forest and no one is there to hear it, it creates a vibration, but no sound.

looked into our cherubic baby faces and said things like, "This is your nose. This is your eye." They could just as well have said, "This is your potato," and our baby brains would have accepted it.

As it turns out, what we experience as "the present" is actually a reality we create by interpreting events and sensations that have been filtered through our past. It just happens so fast we don't catch it.

This is all fine and good with simplistic interactions like, "Please bring home a loaf of bread." What about issues of integrity, honesty, hard work, sensitivity, or customer service? Who looked over our cribs and told us exactly what those terms meant?

And this brings us to the great dilemma. Everyone learned life differently, but we think we all learned it the same. Therefore, when we bump into someone who doesn't open car doors or hold elevators, we assume that they, like we, learned that opening doors and holding elevators is polite, and so we judge them to be intentionally rude and insensitive. Our feelings of frustration and distress signal that our perception of reality is at odds with our belief system about how the world should be.

Perception really is reality.

During my first marriage, I came home from work one day and found my wife using the lavatory in the room adjacent to our closet. I finished hanging up my jacket at the same time she flushed the commode. I followed no more than a step behind her as we both walked toward the master bedroom. At this moment I found myself on the edge of sneezing. I was caught in that awful no man's land of not being able to sneeze and not being able to eliminate the sensation of the impending event. So I started sniffing rapidly. Sniff, sniff, sniff.

My ex-wife stiffened and stopped dead in her tracks. Apparently she interpreted my sniffing as a comment on her personal hygiene. Thankfully, I was able to generate a most satisfying sneeze at that precise moment. Her perception changed, her reality changed with it, and we were both spared an unnecessary confrontation.

What fascinates me about this example is that the pain my ex-wife experienced was real while the conversation that created it was based upon something that was not real. The reason the pain was real was that my wife had experienced real rejection as a part of her personal history. She had experienced rudeness as well. She also had a belief system that people should not be rude to her and they should not reject her. In effect she had created a need to be treated a certain way.

Her interpretation of my sniffing triggered feelings of rudeness and rejection. In that moment she experienced those very real emotions. Now here's where it gets powerful. What if I really *had* intended to be rude and invalidating? She would still have been responsible for her pain, not me. I would be the stimulus and she would still have created the response—in this case pain. (Note: I am not suggesting that abusive behavior is acceptable or to be tolerated, ever.) We create our own emotional and psychological pain based upon how we interpret the world.

There is a way for her to experience my rudeness and rejection and not experience pain. I'll cover that in

Chapter Five. For now, please consider that all emotions are self-generated. Negative emotions are generated when we hold conversations in our heads that trigger existing hurts from our past. Their purpose is to protect us from further pain. These emotions are not something we have, they are something we do. Emotions are the consequence of the conversations we have with ourselves. We do hatred, fear or anger by holding internal conversations about someone or something that we judge to be in violation of our values and beliefs.

In the same way, positive emotions of peace, joy, love, happiness and gratitude are generated when our conversations affirm our values. We create our own happiness!

Because of our unique personal histories and belief systems we interpret our experiences based upon our current awareness.

I believe the conflict we experience in our relationships with other people is perhaps 1 percent the current issue, and 99 percent conflicting personal histories.

When someone at work isn't taking responsibility, we may decide they are lazy. Lazy is a judgement that triggers our personal history regarding laziness. Suddenly we become angry with this irresponsible lazy person. How come when I observe a person acting in a way I call lazy, I'm the one who experiences pain? It is because anger is a secondary emotion designed to protect us or something we value. I interpret this person's behavior as wrong, I identify the person with the behavior and it threatens my beliefs about how the world should be.

Is it possible that "laziness" was not accepted in my personal history? Perhaps I was punished and rejected when I didn't want to do things my father wanted done. I quickly learned that if my desires did not conform to his, my safety, security and acceptance were threatened. Now as an adult, when I observe people "not doing what needs to be done," I activate my past feelings of insecurity and rejection. Of course, this happens so fast, I project that the lazy one is the cause of my pain.

Breakthrough Opportunity

"Two roads diverged in a wood, and I—
I took the one less traveled by, and that has
made all the difference."
                                                    —Robert Frost

If you didn't feel compelled to live up to anyone's expectations but your own . . .

What would you start doing?

_____

_____

What would you stop doing?

_____

_____

What would you continue to do?

_____

_____

I see myself as the victim and I see the lazy person as the perpetrator. In this emotional whirlwind is it any wonder I find it difficult to have a productive conversation with this person?

Consider for a moment that I am not in conflict with this person. Since behavior perfectly reflects an internal conversation, they are doing the only thing they could be doing given their current awareness.

If this is true, it is our personal histories that are in conflict. This clash of personal histories is actually an opportunity to build alignment. Together we can become co-creators of a new conversation that clarifies our expectations and establishes a commitment for how we want things to be.

I don't believe anyone is truly lazy. I believe everyone is motivated. They are simply motivated for their own reasons, not ours. Perhaps an example is in order.

Artists see little point in turning in math assignments. For that matter, they see little value in any assignment unless it involves making a presentation that allows them to express their own ideas and inject ample amounts of humor and maybe play the drums.

Artists have to be extremely resilient to buck a 200-year-old educational system based upon conformity to rules and regurgitation of data. Artists want to create something—not sustain the status quo.

Some teachers and some relatives (operating under their own conversations) felt they would be helping my artistic son by telling him he was lazy and irresponsible. This same kid (who wouldn't bother to turn in assignments he had actually taken the time to complete) would cut sugar and caffeine from his diet and run and bike all summer so he could make the fall soccer team. When all his friends were making plans for college he endured their parent's questions, looks and well-meaning lectures as he outlined his plans to skip college and become a stand-up comic and actor.

When it became clear that his girlfriend's family felt their daughter might want to keep her eye out for a mate who could provide a steady income, he told them, "I'm going to give this career five years, and if I'm not successful I'm going to give it another five."

At age 19 he is doing stand-up three to four nights a week at several venues. He's building contacts, taking classes and having the time of his life. His whole life is possibility.

What emotions were triggered for you as you read my son's story? Did you secretly cheer for him? Did you judge him as lazy? Did you judge me for not setting him straight? What were the conversations that went through your head? What would you say to a son who marched to a different drummer? What did your parents say to you?

Whether you experienced pleasure or pain it was because the story affirmed or threatened your values, beliefs or expectations. Your personal history was activated.

In the next chapters we'll break it down even more clearly. For now, just consider the second law of conscious conversation: our conversations create our own pleasure or pain.

The First Two Laws of Conscious Conversation

1. *Behavior is a perfect reflection of the conversation that created it.*

2. *Our conversations create our own pleasure or pain.*

What beliefs are threatened by the people you least enjoy?

_____

_____

_____

_____

What values are affirmed by the people you most enjoy?

_____

_____

_____

_____

Chapter Three
Understanding Needs

When I was born I didn't have a lot of expectations. I was just grateful for a bigger apartment. At first things were a bit confusing. Really big people kept handing me back and forth while making strange noises. People held me nicely. They smiled and told me I was cute (whatever that meant). If I messed my diapers, people actually fought for the honor of changing them. If I was hungry I would holler and the Mommy person would come and feed me. If I was bored I would holler and the Daddy person would carry me around and show me things. The universe was one big vending machine created for my sole benefit. Life was good.

Then one day the peasants staged a revolution. One morning the Mommy person said, "No!" and she had the nerve to slap my hand! This was the beginning of the end. I could see my whole life pass before my cute little eyes. This had to stop! Civilization as I knew it was hanging by a thread and I had to act fast. My little brain was racing. What always worked in the past? That's it! I'll holler. So I let out a big cry and again reached for the electrical outlet.

Again, the horror! I was not allowed to do what I wanted to do. What ensued is too painful to relate. Suffice it to say we named that period the "terrible twos." I suspect it was because Mom and Dad conspired against me in tandem.

The next few years were a bit unsettling. As you can imagine, it's hard to let go of that much power gracefully. In an attempt to find some safety and security, I developed an unconventional relationship with my right thumb. Mom called it my security blanket. I found I could always feel safe if I had my thumb with me.[1]

At this point I learned a new word: "MINE." I quickly laid claim to everything I could reach. At the grocery store I would feel real pain when mom would replace the cat food I had surreptitiously slipped in the cart. "We don't have a cat!" she would remind me. "Mine!" I would wail. I would throw a full-blown fit in the frozen food aisle if I couldn't have the bag of brussel sprouts I so desperately needed to feel whole. I didn't care if people liked my behavior or not, I didn't want people taking away my stuff.

As I grew older I went to school and made friends. I wanted my friends to like me. I wanted to wear the same clothes they wore. I listened to the same music they listened to and watched the same TV shows they watched. About the age of eighteen I had had enough. My parents had gotten noticeably dense. Hormone levels were dangerously high and I was eager to move out and leave my mark on the world. I wasn't prepared for life but I struck out anyway. Sound familiar?

---

1 I secretly sucked my thumb until I was seven years old. I stopped cold turkey after I read about a thirty two-year-old thumb sucker in *Dear Abby*.

This is the process virtually all humans use to domesticate their young. It is more or less severe in many human cultures, but the pattern is the same. Humans take in excess of 20 years to mature—far longer than any other creature on earth. Along the way different needs arise. If these needs are satisfied, developing humans progress nicely to the next level. If these needs are *not* fully met (a physical example might be a vitamin deficiency in childhood[2]), the adult will often show the consequences.

When we are infants, our primary needs are physical. We need food, shelter, and clothing. Our world revolves around survival.

As we get a bit older our safety and security needs come into play. From the age of about eight or ten through our teenage years, social acceptance becomes a dominant need. This is when kids are most likely to join a gang or change themselves to conform to some other peer group.

Assuming the human's basic acceptance needs are met, her own needs for self-acceptance and self esteem soon take precedence. Ultimately, by her early twenties (assuming all needs have been satisfied thus far), a need to share her unique talents and gifts will emerge.

Human behavior is an attempt to meet a need. By observing the behavior, you can get clues as to what need a person is trying to satisfy.

---

2 Just as a lack of vitamin C causes scurvy and a lack of vitamin D causes rickets, the lack of need satisfaction at certain developmental stages creates a weakness that is triggered by stressful situations. It's akin to taking a drinking straw and bending it. After you straighten it out it looks fine, but if you apply pressure to both ends it will kink in the same spot. When we are under pressure we often default to feelings of rejection or fear or other emotions that represent the need deficiency even though we are not in fact in danger or actually being rejected.

A Man Named Tom[3]

I met Tom when he was in his early 30s. As I shared these ideas a sudden awareness seemed to hit him. "Let me tell you about my childhood," he said. "When I was a little boy, I was one of those kids who lost everything. I'd lose my hat, I'd lose my mittens, I'd lose my school-books. When I was in second or third grade [the age when security and acceptance needs are most present], I lost my mittens at school. This was the third pair of mittens I had lost that year. I was frantically searching everywhere for them, because I knew I'd get in trouble if my Mom found out. When it came time to go home, the principal had to physically put me on the bus because I wouldn't leave without my mittens. On the bus I created a plan. I would sneak into the house and not tell anyone about the lost mittens. The next day at school if I could-n't find the mittens I would go to the lost and found and steal a pair."

With his plan and conversation in place Tom slowly opened the front door of his house and stepped inside. His mother was waiting. "Where are your mittens?" she demanded. "Did you lose them again?"

"No, I didn't lose them."

"Don't lie to me," she said, "You lost them didn't you?"

"No, Mom," he said thinking quickly. "You know how I keep losing my mittens? Well I thought it would be smart to have a school pair of mittens and a home pair of mittens. And since today is the first day of my new plan, I left my mittens at school on purpose!"

---

3 Not his real name.

But she didn't buy it and he finally confessed that he had lost his mittens again.

"Just as I thought," she said reaching for a yellow note pad. She took a pen and wrote on the piece of paper "DO NOT TALK TO ME BECAUSE I AM A LIAR" and she taped it to the front of his snow pants.

Then she took him to the garage and put him in the back seat of the car. She threw in a couple toys and backed out of the driveway. As she circled the neighborhood she said, "Say goodbye."

"Why, Mom, where are we going?"

"Say goodbye," she said, "Because I'm going to take you out in the country and drop you off in a cornfield. I will not have a liar in my house, and no one will take you home either because no one will have a liar in their house."

Tom's experience is known as a significant emotional event.

In that instant his brain created a huge file folder called REJECTION. At his age, rejection was closely related to DEATH. So how did this play out in Tom's life?

Tom pursued a career in sales (can you imagine a career with more rejection?). Tom was always impeccably dressed. He wore three piece suits with watch fobs and collar chains. He smelled of expensive colognes and every hair was in place. He had an uncanny ability to stand much too close to you and almost defy you to push him away. All his body language seemed to scream "Please accept me!"

The career Tom selected was selling expensive men's clothing. He related that he owned 24 suits. Six suits for each season of the year. (This allowed him to wear a fresh suit every day to work plus one for Sunday.) He told me the average cost of each suit was $1000. I asked him how much money he earned selling men's clothing. He said about $2000 per month. Tom had one year's salary hanging in his closet.

We all have a need to feel better. Twenty-four-seven, three-sixty-five.

Breakthrough Opportunity

> *"Know thyself. The unexamined life is not worth living."*
>
> —*Socrates*

If I'm honest with myself and courageous enough to accept the answer, I would say one of my deepest needs is

_____

because

_____

To Tom, feeling better meant being accepted by others. He wanted a closet full of expensive suits because at some level he was telling himself they would make him acceptable.

What makes each of us feel better is related to our unique personal history and the internal conversations we have developed. Imelda Marcos needed 2000 pairs of shoes to feel better. Some people shop till they drop to feel better. I like to go to restaurants and see movies. You may like to rob banks to feel better. But the underlying need is the same.

I was quite agitated when I first was exposed to the idea that my dominant need was as banal as wanting more pleasure and less pain. I had always operated in the belief that humans (and especially me) were built of finer stuff. Then one day I watched Joan Lunden on Good Morning America. Joan looked perfect as always. This particular morning she was interviewing a young woman who was into punk rock. This woman wore black leather and big boots. She had metal studs everywhere and a safety pin through her cheek. Her hair was spiked and tipped with colors not normally found in nature.

Part way through the interview Joan turned to the young woman and said, "I just have to ask you a question. As I look at you I can see you are a very attractive woman." At this point the camera zoomed in for a full headshot. Suddenly, it was easy to see that indeed, this woman was beautiful. Joan continued, "I just have to ask. How come you choose to dress this way?"

Without missing a beat the woman replied, "I'd rather be looked at than overlooked."

Then I got it. I wouldn't pierce myself to feel better . . . but she would. Working with dying people may not be my cup of tea, but it was for Mother Theresa. I don't swear at people to feel better (unless I'm in my car) while others do it quite often. I'm a consultant because it feels better than being a civil engineer. But getting a degree in civil engineering felt better than disappointing my father (who never actually told me I should follow in his footsteps). It felt better to get married at the age of 20 than to let people down, and it felt better to get divorced seventeen years later than to stay married, no matter who I let down.

At each decision point, whether I'm conscious of it or not, I make decisions that are intended to benefit me. Sometimes they bring more pain and regret. Sometimes they work out. In each moment, however, I am only able to make the choice my current awareness presents as a viable option. So our third law of coversation is this: Behavior is an attempt to feel better.

Now here's a powerful and perplexing question. When I choose poorly, am I to blame, or is it my faulty current awareness that is to blame? (Blame is not the same as responsibility—of course I am responsible for my choices.)

Before you answer, consider the plight of those people who engage in a behavior repeatedly, even though they may feel guilty about doing so. They may act promiscuously, abuse alcohol, or lie to their friends. When their current awareness changes and they reflect on their behavior, they promise themselves that it will never happen again. They pray that God will take away their sinful desires. They berate themselves and feel unworthy and incapable of self control. Then—a few hours, days or months later—the old awareness takes over and once again they find themselves loving the very things they say they hate.

I would like to suggest the possibility that when I am most tempted to do the things I hate it is because my mind is on what is wrong or missing in my life. That conversation creates an awareness of how my needs are going unmet and it "kinks my straw." However, when I have a mindset of gratitude, joy or love I am experiencing the sense that all my needs are being satisfied. Consequently I am not susceptible to unhealthy choices masquerading as "feel goods."

The Laws of Conscious Conversation

1. *Behavior is a perfect reflection of the conversation that created it.*

2. *Our conversations create our own pleasure or pain.*

3. *Behavior is an attempt to feel better.*

Breakthrough Opportunity

When I want to feel better, what are the healthy things I do?

_____

_____

_____

_____

What are the unhealthy things I do?

_____

_____

_____

_____

What am I trying to feel when I do the unhealthy things?

_____

_____

_____

_____

What are 3 ways to achieve my desired feelings that support me and my values?

_____

_____

Chapter Four
Value Judgements

When my son was 5 years old he came home from kindergarten all upset. "Dad," he said, "where do babies come from?" This conversation was about 15 years early, from my perspective. Then I remembered the old joke about the father in a similar situation who told his child everything only to hear her say, "Oh, because Mom says they come from the hospital."

Preparing myself for the worst, I asked, "What have you heard?" He proceeded to tell me in quite accurate detail (using both the words "penis" and "vagina" in the correct context) exactly where babies come from. His school bus seat companion was the daughter of a nurse and she had taken it upon herself to share her newfound knowledge with her classmates.

"Well," I said, "you pretty much got it right." He shook his five-year-old head as he looked at the floor. Then he shared his internal conversation. "I just don't see how that would be enjoyable."

Humans tend to judge everything. We constantly criticize, compare and assess. If we stopped the judgement conversation at the level of same/different, useful/not useful, comfortable/not comfortable or even loving/not loving we would live much happier lives.

Unfortunately, we too often take the judgement one step further, to good/bad and right/wrong.

Please let me finish. I did not say there is no such thing as good or bad, right or wrong. I believe evil exists. I am glad we have institutions to incarcerate people who harm others. I believe each of us is responsible for his/her actions and that the consequences of those actions are inescapable. What I am suggesting is that those labels set us up for more pain and less pleasure.

I have found that using these labels usually starts a conversation involving comparison and competition, where someone wins at another's expense.

In the previous chapter we discussed our need to feel more pleasure and less pain. Based on our personal history, we develop our own hierarchy of values along with our own hierarchy of needs. So, when I want to feel better, I may ride my motorcycle at 110 mph. My wife Lisa will listen to her favorite music in front of a fire. My daughter will seek out her best friends to watch a movie and socialize. Each person's value system is an internal source of motivation to select one method of action over another. We are happiest when we live according to our values. Values are affirming to the person who holds them.

Values are also subordinate to needs. By this I mean, if my values say that stealing is unacceptable but I find myself starving to death, my need to live may override my value of honesty. This is an extreme case. How about this: have you ever done something you now regret having done? Does it bother you that you were capable of that behavior? Do you beat yourself up over it and wonder how you can call yourself a good person if you could do that? (Notice that if you aren't a good person then you must be bad and when your current awareness labels you as bad it is very easy to get stuck there.)

Please take a moment and go deeper with me. Think of a time you did something you now regret. At the time you did the thing you now regret, what were the emotions that caused you to do it?

If you are like me and the people in my seminars, you may identify with one or more of the following emotions. Please check off the emotions that were present prior to or during the behavior you now regret.

❏ **Fear**		❏ **Frustration**
❏ **Anger**		❏ **Guilt**
❏ **Rejection**		❏ **Hate**
❏ **Unworthiness**		❏ **Rage**
❏ **Incompetence**		❏ **Helplessness**
❏ **Envy**		❏ **Humiliation**

The fact that you were able to do something you regret suggests you can set aside your own values temporarily.

All too often we misinterpret the purpose of our emotions. Negative emotions are guides, not enemies to be avoided. A feeling of distress tells me my values are being threatened—that I am on the wrong path.

Emotions are like the rumble strips built into the shoulder of a highway. When you start to drift off the main roadway the rumble strips alert you to potential danger. We never drive on rumble strips and then curse the people that built the road. But if we have a relationship that triggers distressing emotions, we routinely blame the other person for "making me feel those rumble strips!"

Negative emotions are painful in order to get our attention and cause us to make a change. We need to take a reality check and respond accordingly.

Too often, instead of choosing a thoughtful response we simply fight back. In my experience this creates more tension, stress and fear. If we were thinking clearly, we would recognize that our actions were bringing more pain, not less, and we would try a different response. But since we think the source of the pain is outside us, it seems reasonable to attack the person we've equated with the pain. If we realized the source of pain was within ourselves, we would become aware of responses that would truly bring resolution.

Consider that strong negative emotions are triggered when we perceive our needs are not being met. Under that extreme emotional pressure we take action designed to meet those needs (even if we must ignore our values to do it).

Then, once our immediate needs are met, our values come creeping back to our consciousness. "Remember me?" they seem to ask. "What were you thinking? How could you do such a thing?"

The human psyche interprets a need as something it can't live without. A want or desire is something that is nice and enhances life but is really more of a luxury than a necessity. Needs, on the other hand, are *critical*.

When our needs are met, we humans tend to be wonderful creatures. We are generous, kind, loving, creative, hard-working, lighthearted, happy, inventive, spontaneous and uplifting. And why not? When our needs are met, our inner conversation tells us that we live in a world of abundance and possibility. We have freedom. We have options, we have choices. In that world, your success does not diminish mine.

When our needs are not met, all bets are off. (When mamma ain't happy, ain't nobody happy.)

Back to values. If we can get our needs met by following our values we are at peace with the world. We sail down the highway of life without a hint of a rumble strip. But what happens if your values are different from mine?

When I notice that your values are different, that part of me that can't seem to stop judging things immediately springs into action. "He thinks it's OK to cheat on his taxes," it might say. "That's wrong, isn't it Mamma? That's bad. That's a bad person, isn't it?" (I'm taking some license with the conversation, but you get the point.) Whether it's taxes, rap music, lifestyles or clothing, we notice and we judge. Then we create a story about the values and the people who hold them that justifies our judgements.

As you can see, when I begin to judge another person's values, I often judge the person as well. I feel better when I judge them wrong or bad, because in so doing I've affirmed my own rightness and goodness. I equate the person with the behavior and the two become inseparable. In my world, the sinner is now the sin, and is equally reprehensible.

What happens when this person is your spouse or child or parent or co-worker? Then what?

Whether you ever tell them or not, people can tell when they've been judged. That's when they pull back. That's when they feel threatened. They may feel guilty, angry, or rejected. They may feel any of the things people feel just before they do something they later regret. And you can bet they will feel a near automatic urge to judge you in return. If that's not a death spiral I don't know what is.

Rather than judging people who have different values, we could accept them. We could accept them and not be threatened by their values if we believed that anyone with their personal history and their hierarchy of needs would have their values and do what they do. (I am not saying it is OK for bank robbers to rob banks, I am saying I can accept that a person's choice to rob a bank is understandable given their personal history, awareness, needs and values. Robbing banks has natural consequences and I support consequences.)

The act of acceptance stops the distress that is caused by actively judging or resisting an unwanted reality. It creates a different conversation. I've come to believe that people are doing the best they can, given their personal awareness and the skills they have at their disposal. Operating under this conversation I quickly see that my parents didn't do anything they need to regret. They were the best parents they knew how to be. If they could have been better I believe they would have been better.

I am the best father I know how to be. Am I the best father in the world? Of course not. But I'm the best me my current skills and awareness will allow.

I believe you are the best mother, father, husband, wife, lover, friend, boss, or employee you know how to be. If you had a greater awareness of how to be better, along with the necessary skill, I believe you would be better. That's the conversation I choose to operate under. It brings me great joy and peace. *The people in my life are doing the only things they could be doing.* The people in my life are always doing their best. What are the people in your life doing?

If the best that people can give is not acceptable, I need to have a conversation with them. I need to bring to their awareness what I would like from them. I don't need to judge them or make them wrong. I don't need to apologize for asking for what I want. I simply ask for it. And based upon the conversation they create around my request, they will honor my request or not.

If you want to better understand the futility of judging others (and free yourself from a lot of stress) complete the following exercise.

Draw a stick figure of a person or situation that triggers negative emotions.

Example:

Describe your judgement in one concise sentence, for example: "Bob is mean to me and makes stupid decisions."

Your judgement:

_____

_____

_____

_____

Now take a solid two minutes and imagine this person or situation in vivid detail. With this picture clear in your mind start telling them off. Call them names, ridicule them, tell them how terrible they are. Keep intensifying your emotions and keep judging them mercilessly for two full minutes, and don't read further until you are done.

After two minutes, most people get bored with the exercise. Aside from initial feelings of power, most people soon realize it is a waste of time. Nothing changes. The person doesn't even know you did the exercise. Judgement changes nothing! That person's awareness is the same as it was before, during and after my ranting. If anything ever is to change, that person will need a new conversation to capture their attention. You'll learn how to have that conversation in chapters 6 and 7.

Let's review the laws of conscious conversation and add one more:

The First Four Laws of Conscious Conversation

1. *Behavior is a perfect reflection of the conversation that created it.*

2. *Our conversations create our own pleasure or pain.*

3. *Behavior is an attempt to feel better*

4. *If people could do better, they would do better.*

These ideas constitute the foundation for a happy and productive life. In the remaining chapters we'll explore how to use these ideas and learn some skills that will allow you to increase your effectiveness.

Chapter Five
The Interpersonal Bridge

A client told me the following story.

Her husband was cleaning out the garage on a sunny Saturday morning in early spring. He had accumulated several large bags of trash. As my client entered the garage to pick out a few gardening supplies, she noticed the growing pile of garbage. "Don't take those out to the curb today," she reminded her husband, "the garbage man doesn't come 'til Thursday and it will look bad to the neighbors."

Without looking up her husband muttered something like "OK, whatever."

Several hours later, her garden nicely prepared, my client hopped in her van and headed to the nursery to pick up the flowers she intended to plant that day. After purchasing several flats of fragile plants, she wheeled her loaded cart to the van, opened up the back and found it stacked full of black garbage bags!

Suddenly a conversation leapt into her head, and she experienced a great deal of anger.

This would be a good time to talk about the concept of the interpersonal bridge.[1]

Up until now we have discussed how each person's personal history comprises all of his or her experiences, needs and values. Our needs are those things we believe are necessary for survival. Our values constitute the way we feel things "should be." We feel comfortable when our values reflect our interpretation of reality, and we feel uncomfortable when our values appear to be threatened.

Together, our needs, values and personal histories create our current awareness and establish our expectations. Our conversations are tightly linked to our expectations. Our expectations become a bridge between ourselves and the other people who are playing through our game of life.

Interpersonal Bridge

When people behave in accordance with my expectations I feel good about our relationship. Trust is the vehicle that rolls back and forth on the bridge. The more we continue to meet each other's expectations the stronger the bridge becomes, and trust flows freely.

Then one day your husband loads your van with garbage bags. He is playing the game wrong. Your expectations have not been met. He didn't behave the way he *should* have.

---

1 For a deeper exploration of the Interpersonal Bridge, read *Shame The Power of Caring,* by Gershen Kaufman.

Missed expectations occur when people don't do what we think they should. Dad doesn't make it to the recital. Mom doesn't buy you the present you wanted for your birthday. Tony doesn't pull his weight on your team projects. Angela doesn't meet you for lunch and doesn't call. Your spouse doesn't listen to you. Your friends don't understand. Each missed expectation looks like a form of rejection.

And it seems to us that our wants, values, and needs are not valid. Then, before we can stop it, a conversation shoots through our synaptic relays. "How come they did this to me? Is it because there is something wrong with me? Don't I warrant their love, acceptance and respect? Don't I matter?"

These conversations create a sharp sense of shame. If our personal history has convinced us that we are indeed incompetent and undeserving, this missed expectation will confirm our self-image and trigger a downward spiral of shame and pain. It can become immobilizing.

If however, our self-esteem is a bit higher, we have a different response. After the initial sting of shame, our psyche rejects the notion that we are wrong to have the expectation, and we instead project some sort of character or competency defect upon the person who is playing the game wrong. My father called these people stupid idiots. The roadways of my childhood were filled with stupid idiots. As a result I am quick to challenge the intelligence of people whose driving isn't up to my standards.

This knee jerk response operates under the conversation that my expectations reflect the way *good* people behave.

Depending upon the severity of the missed expectation, most people will be able to locate themselves on the following scale.

Jerk	Jerk	JERK	JERK
Irritation	Frustration	Anger	Rage

I call it the Jerk Scale. The more enraged I am the bigger jerk you are. (This is wonderfully convenient because it relieves me of personal responsibility when I retaliate.)

Consider the kind of expectations and conversations that could cause a workplace or schoolyard shooting.

The game is even more interesting when one of the rules is "you need to know what I want without my telling you."

One day, in my first marriage, my wife came to me and said, "Bill, you're just not romantic anymore."

"How could this be? I'm still doing the stuff that worked in high school," I thought to myself. "Since when is wanting to make out all the time not romantic?"

But instead of saying that I asked a question. "What's your definition of romantic?" (You see, I was a civil engineer at the time and I wanted to know the formula for romance.)

"If I have to tell you," she said, as she visibly deflated, "it's not romantic."

She expected me to be able to read her mind. (It felt better to her to have a husband who would just know what she wanted. Unfortunately, it felt better to me to avoid conflict and to become silent while expecting her to read my mind as well!)

No one knows what you want until you tell them. And as much as we want to listen to the conversation in our head that says, "If you loved me you'd know what I want," it's not true. It is quite possible to love someone and have no clue as to what they want at any given moment.

Humans are wanting machines. We always want something, and no sooner is that want achieved than a new want surfaces. I'm so hungry I can't see straight, until I eat. Then I'm so thirsty I can't recall being hungry. We hunger and thirst for emotions the way our body yearns for food and water. Our wants change so fast no mortal can be expected to know what someone else wants.

We think we will experience more pleasure if someone meets our needs without being asked. I have to admit, I enjoy those rare occasions when others are living their lives solely to make me happy. I also find that I go a long time between such events if I keep my expectations to myself.

Some people go only halfway. They tell people what they don't like. They talk about how bad a decision is, how thoughtless someone is and how bad so-and-so treats them. They are first-class complainers. In fact, I would say these people don't *have* complaints, they *are* complaints.

Think of the people who have so completely identified with what's wrong in the world that they have become what's wrong. They bring the reality of what's wrong into their awareness. It becomes their prevailing line of thought. As they "awfulize" every situation, they experience the very emotions they say they deplore.

Those of us who live and work with these people soon see them as basically negative. In essence, they have become the complaint. Perhaps an example is in order. Consider the dynamics present in a simple back rub.

Your partner complains of a sore back and you offer a backrub. You sincerely want to be nice and bring her (or him, as the case may be) relief. As you start to work on her shoulders she says "I don't like that." So you move to her middle back. "No, that's not it," she says. You try a different technique. "Nope," comes the response. Three more attempts, three more strikes.

At this point you throw up your arms and say, "Rub your own back!"

Result: Telling people what you *don't* want = no fun for anyone.

Compare that scenario with this. As you start to rub her shoulders she says, "A little softer please." Would you comply? Of course you would. Then a moment later she says, "A little lower and more over my right shoulder blade, please. OK, that's it, right there." Now everyone is having fun. Then something amazing happens. Your partner suddenly says, "OK, now do the other shoulder." What they wanted a moment ago they no longer want. Who could have known?

It's the same at work. Your boss doesn't know what you want or need. Your employees don't know what you want . . . until you tell them.

Now let's go back to the interpersonal bridge. If my expectations aren't met, I am likely to respond with a stage one response and feel shame, or I'll move to stage two and project that the person who let me down is a jerk. Instead of feeling shame, I get to feel angry, lucky me!

There is, however, a third response that does not create pain. In theory a person could move directly to this stage without the pain of the first two conversations. One way to reach the third-stage response requires that I have no expectations at all. I achieve this by eliminating all vestiges of ego. While eastern mystics may achieve this state of consciousness, the Western mind will have a tough go at it.

Another method to get to stage three is to pay attention to any uncomfortable feelings you experience.

When I notice that first sense of pain, or as my wife, Lisa, describes it, "that twisty feeling," I acknowledge it. I may say "ouch!" or, in business settings, I may just silently witness my discomfort. As my mind quickly runs toward the Jerk Scale and begins to label this person, I simply admit that I am now in stage two. "I'm starting to judge them," I may say.

Then I muster my courage and drag my awareness to stage three. Stage three is called "Give love a chance."

Since I'm not a mind reader, I admit that I don't know with complete certainty what *is* actually happening. I simply admit that it is happening and challenge myself to hold love conscious and present in my awareness.

Rather than making assumptions that may or may not be true, I postpone my feelings of anger and move to stage three. I stop myself from making assumptions and start asking questions. I might say, "I need to understand something. How come you put all that garbage in my van?"

This is approximately what happened with the husband and wife in my story. Even though she created a lot of anger and hurt on her drive home, she asked her husband about the garbage before she attacked him.

He said, "That's not garbage. I left the garbage in the garage. Those bags are for the Goodwill. I was going to deliver them this afternoon but you took the van."

The pain she experienced all the way home from the garden center was unnecessary. She did well to ask a question before acting on the conversations in her head. She would have been even happier if she had given love a chance. "Fascinating," she could have said, "I wonder what conversation caused Steve to put these bags in the van?"

Stage one and two responses reflect the classic fight-or-flight responses. We never talk about the third response. Imagine how different our lives would be if we all learned about the fight-or-flight-or-love response. By giving love a chance you escape the painful emotions of stages one and two and instead experience compassion, acceptance and love.

The Fifth Law of Conscious Conversation

Things go better with love.

"You can't always get what you want. But if you try sometimes, you just might find, you get what you need."
—*The Rolling Stones*

Lisa and I enjoy vacationing in Cancun, Mexico. In addition to great weather and beautiful beaches, it has hundreds of places to eat. On vacation we like to eat, walk and enjoy the beach. We are never apart for more than a few minutes in the entire week and we thoroughly enjoy each other's company.

Part of the reason we return to Cancun is because we know what to expect. We know the weather, water and sand will be just as it "should be." We know where to get the best steaks, seafood or music. Some vacations are for exploring new parts of the world. Cancun, for us, is a known quantity of stress-free relaxation and communion.

The only things I've ever found irritating were the time-share salesmen and their relentless attempts to get you into a presentation. It never failed. Lisa and I would be walking hand in hand, deep in conversation when a time-share salesman would thrust himself into our reality uninvited. "Hola! Do you want a free breakfast?" I'd instantly be at stage two. I wouldn't make eye contact, or slow my pace, but just snarl, "We already have plans for breakfast." Of course, the seasoned salesman is more than ready for this. "How about tonight? Would you like a free sunset cruise and lobster dinner?" By now we'd be three steps past his booth strategically placed at the edge of the sidewalk.

"Come here," he'd call out, "let me show you something." "I don't want to see anything," I snap over my shoulder. My jaw would be set, I'd be walking fast and creating my own pain.

By that time the salesman would be on to the next pedestrian and I'd be starting to complain how I wished "those people" wouldn't bother us. After several more run-ins, I made it my mission to put all timeshare salespeople in their place. I decided I would beat them at their own game. I would strike first!

> *"All you need is love."*
> —*The Beatles*

So the next morning as Lisa and I walked arm in arm, deeply in love and enjoying a wonderful personal reality, I saw the salesperson before he saw me. Just as he began to speak I looked him right in the eye and in my best tough-guy voice I said, "I don't want to talk to you!"

"Why not?"

"I don't want to spend my vacation with you, I want to spend it with my wife."

"Would you like to take your beautiful wife to see the dolphins?"

AAAAAARRGHHHHHH!

Never try to beat a timeshare salesperson. They can't hear "no."

After three days of this I was at my wits end. I couldn't think of a single conversation that would get through to these people. And after three days of putting up with my behavior Lisa spoke up. "You know," she said, "with all your complaining, you're starting to sound like your father. Why don't you give love a chance?"

After a brief discussion in which we agreed to never again compare anyone with his or her parents, I agreed with Lisa. What did I have to lose?

I got my chance the next morning. As we approached the salesman I allowed peace and love to swell within me. "He's just trying to make a living," I told myself as I released the tension from my body. "He's being the best salesman he knows how to be."

When he saw me, he noticed my big smile and my relaxed appearance. As he started his sales-pitch, I shook my head slightly and continued smiling as I mouthed the word, "no." His body relaxed; he smiled back and said, "OK."

I couldn't believe it! A surge of happiness flowed through me. This was amazing! All week long I had generated conversations about competition, judgement and comparison. All week long I had lived with the emotions of irritation and anger. By choosing love, I not only received the treatment I wanted, but I got the side benefit of feeling good about how I treated him!

For the rest of the vacation I tried it on everybody. I tried it on the people selling jewelry. I tried it on the T-shirt salesman. Sometimes I even stopped and talked a moment or two so I could practice loving them up close. Finally Lisa asked me to stop loving all those strangers and send some back in her direction.

Not only can you get out of stages one and two by giving love a chance, you can avoid them all together by holding love conscious and present. When you love what is happening and willingly accept the unwanted realities of life, you are at peace. If love is fully present in our awareness, we find ourselves having conversations that become quite hilarious in a good way. We find ourselves saying, "I love life. I love that Michele rolls her eyes at me. I love that Alex won't do his chores. I love that my husband is inattentive."

Now, obviously we don't love those things and that is where the humor lies. Alex isn't going to do his chores, whether we love it or not. People are who they are . . . until they change. When we love them where they are, we don't place barriers in their path that prevent them from becoming who they can be.

The other day I was fascinated as I watched my wife, Lisa. She was deeply focused on some task and unaware of my presence. It dawned on me that I had just caught her in the act of being herself. And she was beautiful. She was solving some problem, making the world the way she wanted it to be and I could see it in her face. She was still eight years old! And so am I. We're all eight years old on the inside. That's why we do what we do. We're just figuring it out the best we can. It's easy to give love a chance when you are offering it to the child inside.

My mother turned 72 years old this year and she shared a secret with me. "I'm still a kid," she told me in a whisper. And as she smiled from the wonder of it I could see the delighted child that lived inside her. When we keep love present and active, we bypass the feelings of rejection and pain. When love is present and active we can imagine the eight-year old in each of us just trying to survive the best way we know how. And we can experience a conversation that creates possibility instead of anger and revenge.

Another strategy to avoid stages one and two is to clarify your expectations in advance. Since both Lisa and I had been married once we had some concerns about getting married again. Did we deserve happiness? Were we lovable? Would we drive each other away? These and dozens of other questions swirled around inside our heads. So during a long car ride to meet a potential client, we decided to voice all of our concerns.

As I drove, Lisa took out her day planner and turned to the note section. Each page received a heading representing an issue we felt had the potential to create strife. We created headings like Money, Housework, In-Laws, Children, Sex, Politics and Religion until we'd included every potentially troublesome issue we could imagine. Each page was divided in half. One half was for me and one half for Lisa. Each half was divided again into a section for needs and a section for wants. It looked like this:

Issue: Pets

Bill's Needs	*Lisa's Needs*
I need to feel free to travel without being tied down by pets.	I need to have animals in my life.

Issue: Pets

Bill's Wants	Lisa's Wants
No pets in the bedroom	Four horses, one dog and a maximum of two cats.
No pets on furniture	
No ruined carpet, shoes, etc.	
I'm comfortable with one or two horses and one dog.	

In essence we created a pre-nuptial agreement describing what we could expect from each other. We created the rules to our own game.

We agreed that our needs were critical for our physical and emotional well-being and that wants were desirable but optional.

Over the next three and a half hours we talked through every point. We explained how our personal histories had brought us to need and want certain things. As we understood each other's past, each request became logical, and we found that we were happy to help each other get our needs met.

About twice a year we look at the list. Actually, Lisa reviews it and tells me she is in full compliance. For example, in the pet category, it turns out (she tells me) that if an animal should have a baby or if a pet is purchased for the sole purpose of being a companion to an existing pet, then technically the second animal belongs to the first animal and does not violate the maximum-number-of-pets-agreement. That's why we now have 4 horses, 2 dogs and 3 cats.[2] It should be noted that just because someone needs or wants something doesn't mean you have it to give. I recommend taking a few minutes to determine what you have to bring to a relationship.

Are you great at humor but terrible at compassion? Is it easy or hard for you to give a compliment? Do you like freewheeling abstract conversations, or do you feel most comfortable talking about specific and knowable facts?

Once you are clear on what you have to give, figure out what you need *from* a relationship. Do you need to feel respected? Intelligent? Unique?

Now you are in a position both to decide whom you wish to have in your life, and to define the nature of each relationship.

Perhaps your partner meets certain needs and misses on others. Certain friends will supply the missing needs just as you supply needs for them. It's all good. You can release your need to get love from someone who can't give it and be comfortable in their presence. Why make two people miserable by demanding something they don't have to give?

---

2 Clearly needs and wants change over time. That's why it is so important to revisit the exercise, speak up and clarify expectations. I've found that I enjoy our animals much more than I thought I would and that my real need of being able to travel without worry was met when we found a great kennel our dogs actually like!

Example:

Things I don't bring to a relationship	Things I bring to a relationship	Things I want in a relationship
I have to work hard at:	It is easy for me to:	I want to feel:
• Intuiting what people want	• Verbalize appreciation	• respected
• Asking for help	• Be affectionate	• desirable
• Understanding my feelings	• Be happy	• capable
• Being tolerant of people who are not self-reliant	• Help people who take responsibility for their actions	I want someone who:
	• Let others make their own decisions	• has dreams and goals
		• is authentic
		• is passionate about life
		• is comfortable with themselves

One final thought. I mentioned earlier that one way to avoid making assumptions is to ask questions. When Lisa and I first got together each of us would unknowingly do things that would trigger painful memories about the other's previous partner. To avoid assumptions and unnecessary pain, we invented a mechanism to ask for clarity without aggravating the situation.

The person whose memory is getting triggered raises an index finger as if to ask a question and says, "Inquiry." At this signal, we are allowed to ask how to interpret a particular action or statement of the other person.

For example, Lisa might say, "Inquiry. When you made that observation about that driver, were you trying to tell me you don't like the way I drive?" By a simple inquiry she can find out what I am trying to communicate. She may find I meant no harm or she may cause me to be more honest and clearly make a request. At the very least, use of this mechanism challenges me to evaluate my behavior and make a new choice if I desire. (I love it when Lisa challenges me!)

If you want to try this for yourself, just start reminding yourself to give love a chance and ask a question.

Chapter Six
Changing the Game

Let's review our key points:

Conscious Conversation Laws

1. Behavior is a perfect reflection of the conversation that created it.

2. Our conversations create our own pleasure or pain.

3. Behavior is an attempt to feel better.

4. If people *could* do better, people *would* do better.

5. Things go better with love.

I believe that living under these conversations will eliminate most of the pain from your life. You will also find that the people who agree to use these laws with you become willing partners in the reality you are creating, and it will be more fun than you can imagine!

I get secretly excited when Lisa and I disagree. I look forward to resolving the issue and the freedom that inevitably comes out of the conflict. I don't interpret what we do as conflict resolution; I feel we are aggressively creating alignment.

Before I met Lisa, I avoided anger and conflict. It terrified me. I didn't understand it. I had no models for it. If someone got angry, I took it personally. I stayed in stage one or two, and I wouldn't ask for what I wanted. That all changed when I married Lisa.

Lisa creates a safe place of acceptance that allows me to ask for what I want. In return, I feel no desire to change Lisa. I married all of her and I have chosen to love all of her. Our disagreements take on the tone of trying to understand each other and establishing new expectations to make the game more fun. We don't just resolve conflict; we create a game we both want to play.

Here's how we play the game. As I wrote the last sentence, my cell phone beeped indicating I had a message waiting. It was Lisa. She started her message like this: "Hello, the perfect love of my life!" She then let me know of a person I needed to reach today. She ended her call like this: "I'm looking forward to seeing you when you get home. I'm extra snuggly and I'd enjoy being with you right now. See you later, bye."

Those words bring up all kinds of fun feelings. Both of us take responsibility for creating and re-creating a reality of respect, acceptance, honor and love. Sometimes we slip. If we remember to give love a chance, we rebound quickly. If we hang out in stage one or two for a while, inevitably one of us realizes we are playing a game that isn't fun. So we change it.

This chapter is about ways to change the game. Once again, I'll turn to my children for an example.

But first, a little background. One of the peak experiences of my life began with a two-day workshop on self-esteem. The concept that stood out above all others was the concept of Total Unconditional Acceptance. The idea is not exactly new, but I found myself enthralled with the possibilities of truly living a non-judging life. To discipline myself and to expand my awareness I had a watch made with the initials TUA boldly printed on its face. Now for the story . . .

One early Father's Day morning I was startled awake. My eyes popped open to see my son's face about 6 inches from mine. "Happy Father's Day, Dad."

"Happy Father's Day, Justin." I replied as I allowed my heart rate to drop back under 120.

"Here's your present!" he crowed as he handed me a brand new basketball. "And there's more!" he said leading me to the garage where we discovered a very large box containing a basketball backstop just begging to be assembled. "Isn't it great, Dad? It's even adjustable. You can lower the basket all the way down to 5 feet!"

The next few hours were a flurry of buying concrete, reading directions and digging a 3-foot hole. Justin hovered around each step.

When we started to mix the concrete I realized I was wearing my TUA watch, so I gave it to Justin and asked him to put it inside our car where it wouldn't be damaged. Justin solemnly took off his $2 Superman watch and took both watches over to the car. I happened to look over just in time to see him lay both watches on the hood of the car.

I felt stress.

"That's not what I asked!" I thought. "He's not obeying me. I'm his father; he's supposed to obey me. What would happen if we forget about the watches and drive off?" Clearly I had some unspoken expectations that Justin wasn't following.

I was at a low-level stage 2 when I thought, "This is a teachable moment. I won't make a scene now, but when we're done and we are retrieving the watches I'll remind him of my request and ask what would have happened to the watches if we had forgotten them. He'll see that my request was wise and good and he'll learn a nice lesson. I will be PSYCHOLOGY DAD!"

As we worked with the concrete I turned all my attention to the task at hand. About the time I finished and started cleaning up, Justin retrieved his watch and ran off to play. Of course I forgot about my watch altogether.

Then I decided it would be a good time to mow the yard. So I backed the car out of the way to get at the lawnmower. After the yard, I decided the bushes needed trimming. I played weekend warrior all day and never once remembered my watch was sitting on the hood of my car.

Just before bedtime I remembered that my car was still sitting outside, so I zipped it around the circle driveway and parked it in the garage.

The next morning as I was getting ready for church I realized I couldn't find my watch anywhere. I looked over at Justin to see him carefully strapping his Superman watch to his wrist.

"Have you seen my watch, Justin?"

"No, Dad. Didn't you get it off the car?"

"AAAARRGGHHH!"

We both ran outside to look for it. I went one way around the circle and Justin went the other. It had rained all night and our red rock driveway was now a mixture of gravel and puddles. I happened across the watch first and, though it was a bit soggy and dirty, it was unharmed.

Justin was quickly at my side, looking up with his eyes wide and concerned. "Is it OK, Dad?" he said as if it were a living thing.

"THINK, THINK, THINK!" I said to myself.

"Yes, it's fine." I said as I carefully planned my next sentence.

"Oh, good," he sighed.

"You know, Justin, I asked you to put my watch inside the car."

"Yeah," he said as he lowered his eyes.

"And instead you put it on the hood."

Another "Yeah," a note lower and softer.

"I have to admit," I said, "when I saw you put it on the car I felt stress."

"Yeah," he said again, his whole body sinking.

"Well," I began, "let that be a lesson to us . . ." but before I could finish, Justin quickly brightened. "Yeah," he said, looking up, "Next time you feel stress, speak up!"

If you want a better result you have to be willing to change the game.

Breakthrough Opportunity

The Game you've been playing:

Objective:

_____

_____

Rules:

_____

_____

Strategies:

_____

_____

The Game that excites you:

Objective:

_____

_____

Rules:

_____

_____

Strategies:

_____

_____

Changing the Game with a Relationship:

1. I want to improve my relationship with:

   _____

2. I want to change the following results I currently experience in this relationship:

   _____

   _____

   _____

3. I find myself holding back by:

   _____

   _____

   _____

4. I could create different results by letting go of:

   _____

   _____

   _____

5. Comments/insights:

   _____

   _____

   _____

6. Actions I can take:

   _____

   _____

   _____

Distress or pain is the signal that means "Warning, sensors have detected a potential threat to the game! Take action."

But what action should we take? We all take some action already. We get a stomachache. We yell. We tell stories in our head. We have a hundred and one private conversations that do nothing to alleviate the pain. The trick is to change the game and live out loud. Acknowledge the discomfort, make a request, or ask a question, but at least speak up!

Babies are great at this. When a baby messes its diapers it lets the whole universe know. "Hey, I've got a problem here. This is not how I want to live my life!"

What do adults do? They try to fit in. They avoid conflict. If they can't say anything nice they say nothing at all. They don't let you see them sweat. They grin and bear it. In essence, they lie. They put on the mask and go to stage two.

When adults get a load in their britches they don't speak up . . . they just walk funny.

Look at all the people at work who walk funny. You know they're carrying a load, but they won't let you be part of the solution. They think people are the problem, so they suffer. And they get ulcers and they mope around and they create their own pain because it feels better than confronting the situation and creating a new game, and they stay stuck for years.

Take a lesson from my son. When you feel stress, speak up.

Here are two ways to do it. First, acknowledge the game by noticing your discomfort. Then:

1. Make a request or

2. Ask open-ended questions and then make a request

Your request might sound like this:

> "I'm feeling uncomfortable. Would you speak more slowly and softly please?"

Or you might say,

> "I'm starting to think you want me to feel guilty. Will you please tell me what you want?"

Or how about this:

> "When you allowed the boss to think I had made the mistake I felt betrayed. The next time we work together, I need you to take responsibility for your part."

A more positive example could sound like this:

> "Sweetheart, I'm feeling sad about our fight. I want to be able to talk about things without either of us feeling put down. How would you like me to bring up sensitive issues in the future?"

The basic model is comprised of two simple steps:

1. Acknowledge my feelings.

2. Request what I want.

Even if you don't state your feelings out loud, I encourage you to identify them. Feelings are messengers and they keep pounding on the door until you admit they exist.

Open-ended questions take some practice to master. It is worth it. I owe my relationships, my consulting success, my personal sense of effectiveness and my better than 90% closing ratio to asking questions people want to answer.

The questions that will resolve conflict, create alignment and spur action are questions focused on solutions, on the future and on possibility.

Salespeople will remember the old adage; "Tellin' ain't sellin'. Asking questions is." Not the best grammar, but it does stick in your mind.

There's another reason I ask solution-focused questions. People don't argue with their own solutions. When I ask solution-focused questions the answers people offer reflect *their* values, *their* needs, *their* wants.

However the most important reason I ask solution-focused questions is because they create feelings of high self-esteem. People experiencing high self-esteem feel capable and worthy.

If we've established that people do things for their reasons, not ours, then how can we expect people to try on a new behavior unless they believe it will bring them more pleasure and less pain?

When I ask my clients to list the behaviors they want to eradicate from their organizations and what behaviors they would like to see replace them, they typically generate the following type of lists.

Undesirable behaviors	Desirable behaviors
Selfishness	Responsible/ accountable
Blame	
Gossip	Helpful
Lack of urgency	Keeps promises
Tardy/absent	Creative
"not my job" attitude	Compassionate
Arrogant	Big-picture thinker
Rude	Energetic
Intimidating	Diplomatic
Negative	Honest
	Gets things done

It's important to note that these lists do not describe US and THEM. Hopefully we all hang out on the right side of the chart, but sometimes we slip. So the chart reflects humans, not classes of people.

Think about the conversations that must be going through the mind of a person who is selfish and blaming. This person gossips, lacks urgency, comes late, and doesn't accept ownership. He or she may be arrogant, rude, intimidating and negative.

Is it fair to say that at some deep level these behaviors give insight into how this person feels? Most people agree they do. In the same way, due to a very different conversation, people are motivated to declare themselves accountable, to help others, keep promises and practice the other wonderful behaviors. Can we also suspect these positive behaviors give insight into how these people are feeling?

I believe we can. Therefore, the challenge is this: if we have conversations with people who exhibit undesirable behavior and we ask them to start behaving differently, but they don't feel significantly different as a result of the conversation, what are the odds they can sustain the new behavior?

ZERO.

That is the flaw in most development plans and performance reviews: they try to make people change behavior without considering what people are, and what they want. It is critical that the people we hope to enroll in this new game feel both capable of changing and worthy of the rewards the change will bring. They have to desire the emotion the new game promises to give them.

They have to want to change.

Therefore, getting what you want is an outcome of helping others get what *they* want. And as my daughter fully knows, it is not what you ask for, but *how* you ask for it that makes all the difference. If you want wonderful relationships, make it a practice to reward people for "doing business" with you. Let me tell you about Matthew.

To celebrate my daughter's graduation from college and to keep my promise to myself to take one week off every quarter, we decided to go to Barbados. (I can't tell you too much about Barbados because I don't want it all flooded with tourists the next time I go back.)

About two days into the vacation, Melissa and I were sunning on the beach. Shortly after Missi went inside to cool off, Matthew walked up. Matthew's shirt was unwashed and too big for his thin body. His baggy shorts hung from bony hips and three of his front teeth were missing. He wore his short hair twisted into small dreadlocks. Matthew was a beach vendor.

"Hey, mon."

"Hello."

"My name is Matthew."

"Hi, Matthew, I'm Bill."

"Hello, Bill, welcome to my office," he says, with a sweeping gesture that redirects my view to the cobalt ocean and incredibly white beach.

"You know," he continues, "the sun can be very hot. Dat woman who was with you earlier, her skin is very fair." Matthew is now sitting on the foot of my recliner. "Yes, that was my daughter."

"Yah, her skin is very fair; I have something to cool her skin so she can enjoy Barbados." Matthew pulls out some Aloe Vera leaves. "I can make a special lotion. Very good for da skin." Then, noticing the scar from my bypass surgery, Matthew adds, "You rub some on your scar and it will go away."

I look in Matthew's eyes. He is not putting me on. He believes every word and is genuinely concerned for my scar and my fair-skinned daughter.

"Here," he says, "try some." I watch closely as he selects a stalk of aloe and cuts off a section about an inch long.

Using a butter knife, he turns the gel inside into a slurry and pours it into my hand. He motions for me to rub it on my chest and shoulders. His expression is one if anticipation and confidence. He had done this before.

Of course I rub it on. Of course it feels wonderful. Just as Matthew said it would. (How could anything in Matthew's office feel bad?)

"I'll make a bottle for you so you can enjoy your vacation." I bite. "How much is a bottle?"

"20 dollars Barbados. But don't worry, if you have no money on da beach. I give you da bottle and when you have money you find me and pay me den." (Can you see how Matthew is building our interpersonal bridge by extending trust before I've earned it?)

Matthew then proceeds to make up a bottle of pure Aloe Vera with a flourish that would put the most theatrical shoe-shine vendor to shame. Pieces of aloe are dispatched with the efficiency and dramatic effects of a maestro conducting the Philharmonic Orchestra as the slimy goo is juggled and chased and somehow funneled into an empty seven-ounce Barbados Rum bottle.

It doesn't take a genius to figure out I just spent $10 for two Aloe Vera leaves.

Matthew is beaming. I don't notice the missing teeth anymore. He hands me the bottle. I attempt to shake his hand but he just makes a fist and aims his knuckles straight at me. His eyes say "This is how we do it here."

So I make a fist and from a distance of about 2 inches we accelerate our fists and wrap knuckles. "Respect," says Matthew as he rises and leaves.

I'm surprised at how hard we wrapped knuckles. The sensation lingers for over a minute. I am now the proud owner of seven ounces of aloe goo. And I feel happy and cared for and trusted and respected. Not bad for ten dollars U.S.

Matthew knows how to reward people for doing business with him.

Find ways to reward people for treating you the way you like to be treated. And remember, it only feels like a reward if it gives *them* the feeling they value. Help them *want* to change the game.

The technique you are about to learn will help you uncover what people really *want* to do. It will help you find points of synergy and mutual benefit.

Please think of a problem you currently face. (It is critical that you actually do this. By keeping a real problem in your mind as I ask you a few questions, you'll experience something that will make you a true believer.)

Keep the problem in mind and read each of the following questions. After reading a question, allow your mind to answer it fully before you read the next question. When you finish, read the instructions on the next page.

1. What's wrong?

2. Why do you have this problem?

3. Whose fault is it?

4. How long has this been going on?

5. What is this problem costing you?

6. Why haven't you overcome it?

Please take a moment and write down the feelings and emotions you experienced as you read these problem-focused questions.

Most people experience feelings of guilt, anger, frustration, fear, blame, being stuck and rejection. A very small percentage feel a sense of clarity and relief.

Please notice that the feelings these questions trigger are often close cousins to the feelings we identified as present when we did something we now regret (fear, anger, rejection, unworthiness). Wild, isn't it?

Now let's explore a more useful approach. Please take a moment to release the feelings this first exercise triggered. (Feel free to take a cleansing breath to allow your body to relax a bit.)

In a moment I'll ask you to read a different set of questions. For these questions I want you to think about the same problem you used before. This time, however, you may wish to re-frame it and call it an issue or situation. Some people may prefer to call it a challenge.

The first question you'll be asked to answer is "What do I really, *really*, want?" This question is very different from "What's wrong?" Please listen to each question with fresh ears and don't allow yourself to simply repeat the answers from the first exercise.

One more thing. Question #4 asks you to consider your resources and/or options. This may mean listing the people you know who know someone who can help you. Please take your time to think through these options.

When you're ready please begin.

Regarding the challenge you currently face:

1. What do you really, *really* want?[1]

2. When do you want it?

3. What has to happen for you to get it?

4. What resources and options are available to you?

5. How can you best utilize each resource or option?

6. What can you begin doing now to get what you want?

---

1 I learned the concept of solution focus questions from Michael Wickett, author of, *Its all Within Your Reach*.

Now, write down the feelings and emotions this conversation created in you.

_____

_____

_____

_____

_____

_____

_____

_____

_____

_____

_____

_____

_____

Most people list very positive emotions like empowered, excited, hopeful, optimistic, and clear.

Even though someone will occasionally say these questions triggered more anxiety than the first set, the vast majority greatly prefer solution-focused questions.

Let's examine what just happened. In less than 4 or 5 minutes you may have found yourself with a significant mood swing. How come? How did solution-focused questions do it?

First notice that problem-focused questions are positioned in the past. As Dr. Phil[2] says, "Even God can't change the past." Possibility exists only in the future.

Second, notice that several problem-focused questions start with "why." Many people hear "why" as an attack they must defend. "Why did you do that?" implies the unstated attack, "You idiot." On the other hand, solution-focused questions imply capability, possibility and worth.

"What do you want?" implies you can get it and you deserve it. "What resources or options are available?" tells your brain you have choices. The process of enrolling people in a new game is the process of helping them design it themselves.

Some years ago Peter Senge wrote a book called *The Fifth Discipline*. To me his basic message is embodied in the statement that "Your organization is perfectly designed to give you the results you currently experience." I think we can take it further. I believe your life is designed to give you the results you currently experience. Your family, your relationships, your church, your schools, your hobbies are all perfectly designed to give you the results you currently experience. To me this boils down to the following thought.

Your conversations are perfectly designed to give you the results you currently experience. Our lives are a perfect reflection of our conversations.

Future-focused, solution-focused, and possibility-focused questions create a new conversation. They design a new game.

---

2 Dr. Phil McGraw, author of *Self Matters*

One more kid story.

One evening I came home from work to find my son lying on the couch literally moaning out loud. He was playing the victim card big time. He was one moment away from saying, "Woe is me!"

As I filtered his behavior though my past, I heard myself starting to utter an echo of my father's words. I caught myself a split second before I let my father say through me, "What's the matter with YOU?"

That would have been a problem-focused question. It's pretty difficult to recover from a question like that.

So I asked a different question that created possibilities. The exchange went like this:

Justin:	(moaning)
Me:	Justin, what are a couple things you'd enjoy doing right now?
Justin:	What? (no longer moaning)
Me:	What would you prefer to be doing right now?
Justin:	I'd like to play catch. Want to play with me?
Me:	Sure, mind if I change first?
Justin:	OK, I'll get all the stuff ready.

And in a second he was digging gloves and a ball out of the hall closet. As I changed my clothes I asked myself, "Is it really that easy?"

It's that easy.

In my seminars there are occasionally a few people who feel anxiety when they hear this story. "But what was wrong?" they want to know. "His game wasn't any fun," I say. "He was operating under a conversation that created pain. I invited him to create a new game. His new game enrolled me as a co-creator. I don't think anything was wrong."

Some people love that answer. Some people hate it. Their conversations are perfectly designed to give them that result.

Chapter Seven
WWIINN™ Conversations

The previous chapter underscores a powerful premise. It suggests that our thoughts create our feelings, not the other way around. Our feelings cause us to take action all the while our thoughts are creating the emotions. This is consistent with our previous discussion of how our interpretation of reality becomes our reality.

If people fully understood this relationship bumper stickers all over America would change. Instead of announcing "I'd rather be sailing" or "I'd rather be golfing" the new stickers would say, "I'd rather be thinking something else." We change our emotions by changing our conversations.

In the previous chapter we experienced the way solution-focused questions have the ability to change our emotional state almost immediately. They work wonderfully when the other person is willing to answer them and when you do not have a specific outcome in mind. What happens when you have an outcome you really hope to reach? Perhaps it is not acceptable that a co-worker uses certain language in your presence. Perhaps an employee is chronically late or her performance is unacceptable. Perhaps your Mother-in-law does or says things every Thanksgiving that leave you feeling incompetent or shamed.

In those situations you may find that WWIINN™ coaching provides a mechanism that will allow you to design a game you can both enjoy.

WWIINN™ coaching is a "power-with" conversation, not "power-over." Power-over conversations are parent/child or boss/subordinate type conversations that employ positional power and implied threat to be effective. WWIINN™ coaching[1] relies on your power and right as a human being to ask for what you want. As a power-with approach, it also acknowledges the other person's rights and dignity. WWIINN™ coaching enrolls the other person and views him or her as part of the solution, not the problem.

Here's what **WWIINN™** stands for:

W: What do I really, really **w**ant?

W: What have I **w**itnessed?

I: What is the **i**mpact?

I: Use "**I**" statements.

N: What I **n**eed from you is . . .

N: What do you **n**eed from me to be able to do that?

---

1 To receive a free WWIINN Coaching pocket card, visit our website at wwiinncoaching.com.

When people share their fear of confronting someone, they often say they don't know what to say and they are afraid the other person will get defensive. Some people are afraid they'll get flustered and give up before they can finish. Asking people to change their behavior triggers lots of conversations from our personal history, especially if we see it as confrontation. WWIINN™ coaching helps you stay on track and it minimizes defensiveness.

Let's try it out on the following scenario.

I was sitting at a college football game watching the Minnesota Gophers get annihilated by Michigan. Two young boys sat directly behind me. Not only did they bump my head around as they went back and forth to the food stands and bathrooms every few minutes, but when they finally sat down they spent the majority of the time kicking the back of my chair.

I became irritated. When I would glance over my shoulder all I saw was a very big father who looked like he was no stranger to confrontation.

I decided to tolerate the kicking.

At some point in an abusive relationship, it becomes clear that the victim colludes with the victimizer to keep the abuse alive. I call it "What I allow, I teach." The longer I allowed the boys to invade my space, the more I was teaching them to be insensitive and unaware.

I gave love a chance. I knew these boys were not attacking me personally. They were simply operating under an awareness that did not include me.

Breakthrough Opportunity

*We teach people how to treat us by what
we allow.*

Who have I allowed to treat me poorly?

_____

_____

What have I done or not done to teach them I
would accept their behavior?

_____

_____

_____

What specifically would I like them to start doing
or stop doing?

_____

_____

_____

What would I be willing to do for them if they
would do these things for me?

_____

_____

_____

"Hey, guys," I said in a happy, non-threatening voice as I
watched their father out of the corner of my eye, "Are
you enjoying the game?" They nodded yes and immedi-

ately stopped bumping me. "I want to enjoy the game, too," I said, stating what I wanted. "Will you please be careful not to bump my chair?"

They both nodded their heads and sat up straight in their seats. Their father relaxed and my chair was bump-free the rest of the game.

In this case I didn't feel I needed to hit every point of WWIINN™ coaching so I just stated what I wanted and made my request.

In more complex situations I use all the steps.

Here's a great example. Today I'm writing this chapter at the local Starbucks® coffee shop. One of the employees has asked her boyfriend to hang out at the store until she finishes her shift. He's been quietly doing paperwork and reading. In between customers his girlfriend will come by and check in. They seem happy. He's sitting about three feet from me so I can't help but hear everything they say. (Besides, I'm a huge voyeur.)

A few minutes ago he got a call on his cell phone. A friend who rarely gets to town is in the neighborhood and has invited our hero to watch a game with him that begins at 2:30. That gives him 15 minutes.

"I can't do it," he tells his friend. "I promised Jenny I'd hang with her." After a pause he then says, "OK, I'll ask her and call you back."

Our hero then walks over to Jenny and tells her about his invitation. I can't read lips, but I can tell he's not getting the answer he wants.

Soon he's back on the phone. "It's me. I can't do it. I have to take Jenny somewhere when she gets off work." Imagine the emotions that conversation is creating for our hero. "I can't" and "I have to" is classic victim language. He's creating a conversation that implies he is powerless and Jenny has all the control.

When he hangs up Jenny comes over to his table to defend herself. "You promised you would spend the day with me," she reminds him, as her interpersonal bridge starts to creak.

"I know, but I can be with you anytime, and he hardly ever comes home," whines our hero as he digs his own grave with his words.

I edge my chair closer and appear to be fascinated with a rogue hangnail as Jenny responds.

"We said we'd go shopping."

Taking no responsibility and making no request, Hero digs himself deeper.

"But he wants me to come!"

"And I want you to stay!"

"What do you *really* want?" I think.

The next forty-five minutes consist of pain and anguish as our star-crossed lovers wrestle with everything but what's really going on.

Jenny wants to feel important, accepted and loved. Hero avoids conflict by trying to please everyone. He is bored out of his mind and feels trapped. The more Jenny insists he keep his promise to stay the more he feels controlled. They are both firmly stuck in stage two. Missed expectations are now being interpreted by each of them as character defects in the other.

At 3:00 Jenny gives him the old "If you want to go so bad, just go."

"It's too late," he says, again avoiding all responsibility while slinging guilt.

Five minutes later, Hero is walking out the door. He is staring at Jenny who does not make eye contact. As he passes her she stares at him all the way to the parking lot. He never looks back.

Imagine what playing that game will produce. Each thinks the other is to blame for their hurt feelings. If they knew they were creating their own game, they could have used a different conversation to get all their needs met. It might have gone like this:

Hero: Jenny, I just got a call from Tony. He's back in town for the weekend and he's invited me to watch the basketball game at 2:30.

Jenny: I thought we were going to spend the day together.

Hero: I know, and I really want to spend time with just the two of us. I thought it would be fun to wait here and read, but you don't get off till 5:00 and I'm really bored.

Jenny: What are you thinking?

Hero: I want to hang out with Tony until 4:30. Then I'd like to come back here and we can still go out at 5:00.

Jenny: This feels like Tony is more important than I am.

Hero: I can understand how it could feel that way, and that's not the case. I love you, sweetheart; I'm just feeling bored. I thought when I agreed to come to work with you that we'd have more time to talk.

Jenny: It has been busier than normal today and I haven't been able to hang out with you as I'd hoped. How about this: after you see Tony let's rent a movie. I just want to crash tonight and snuggle on the couch, OK?

I think it's safe to say our hero would have been very willing to accommodate Jenny's request. They obviously care for each other. Jenny certainly doesn't want him to feel boredom or resentment because the original game wasn't working. And Hero doesn't want Jenny to feel rejected. Since they didn't have that conversation, here's how they could use a WWIINN™ conversation to get back in alignment.

Reconciliation Scenario 1: Hero uses WWIINN™

(W) Hero: Jenny, our relationship is very important to me. I love you and I want to make up.

Jenny: If it's so important, why did you stand me up for Tony?

(W) Hero: That's what I want to talk about. When I told you Tony wanted me to come over you said I shouldn't even ask because I had already promised to wait for you.

Jenny: Well, you shouldn't have. If you had just kept your promise none of this would have happened.

(I) Hero: I agree we wouldn't have argued if I had kept silent, and yet I want to feel I can share everything with you. When you told me I shouldn't have asked, I felt controlled. I began to think you didn't care about my feelings and I got angry.

Jenny: You made me mad when you changed the plan.

(I) Hero: I know unexpected changes can be upsetting. I was upset, too, and to avoid hurting each other in the future, I have a request.

Jenny: What?

(N) Hero: The next time I want to make a change in plans, I want to feel free to discuss it openly. How would you like me to bring it up?

(N) Jenny: I would like you to tell me what *you* want to do. You told me Tony wanted you to come over. It seemed like you were blaming Tony.

Hero: I'll do my best to speak for myself. I really did want to see Tony but I didn't want to tell you I was bored sitting here.

Jenny: Why didn't you tell me you were bored?

Hero: I didn't want you to feel bad for me, and until Tony called it wasn't all that bad.

(N) Jenny: In that case I also have a request. A few minutes before Tony called I asked how you were doing and you said fine. If you had told me you were bored I would have encouraged you to see Tony. I need you to tell me the truth. I can handle it.

(N) Hero: Fair enough. I'll speak for myself and I'll tell you how I'm feeling. But if I tell you something you don't want to hear, please don't take it personally.

Jenny: It's a deal.

Reconciliation Scenario 2: Jenny uses WWIINN™

Jenny: Hero, can we talk for a moment?

Hero: Sure.

(W) Jenny: Hero, I feel bad about our fight. I love you and I want to figure out ways to communicate better.

Hero: OK.

(W) Jenny: When you agreed to wait for me at work, I felt very special and loved. I was also concerned you weren't having fun because I couldn't spend much time with you. Then when you told me Tony wanted you to go see a game I felt like you really didn't want to be with me.

Hero: That's not true.

Jenny: I understand that, and yet, at the time that's how I interpreted it.

Hero: I'm sorry.

(I) Jenny: I'm just letting you know what was going on. Then, when I reminded you of our plans, you said Tony really wanted you to come see him. I interpreted that to mean you were afraid to tell me what you wanted, and I got angry and I wanted to punish you for not speaking up.

Hero: Wow.

(N) Jenny: The next time you're feeling bored or you want to do something other than we've planned, I need you to feel comfortable speaking up. What do you need from me to be able to do that?

(N) Hero: Sometimes I don't speak up because I'm afraid you'll take it personally. If I want to see Tony it's not because I care any less about you. Tony and I have been best friends since fourth grade. When he comes back from college I hate to miss him. I'll speak up if you'll agree not to take it personally.

(N) Jenny: How about this: if you feel uncomfortable speaking up you could say "I want to say something, but I don't want you to take it personally." Then I won't. OK?

Hero: It's a deal.

WWIINN™ conversations allow you to stay on track and simply ask for what you want.

You may have noticed in both scenarios that sometimes your partner may still be angry or defensive. They may try to use guilt to their advantage, or they may interpret things differently than you intend them.

An example from Scenario 1 was when Jenny said; "If you had just kept your promise, none of this would have happened." Our hero was able to navigate that sidetrack without offending her or triggering more defensiveness. He did it by validating Jenny's point of view.

I call this verbal Judo. The art of Judo is the art of using your opponent's strength and momentum to your advantage. Rather than resisting an opponent's strength, the Judo master moves in concert with the attacker and then redirects his or her energy.

Don't use verbal sumo, it's not pretty and it doesn't work. Verbal judo directs the energy towards alignment and resolution.

If a person tried to strike you, imagine how easily he would lose his balance if you caught his fist and pulled in the direction of his swing. His whole body would lurch forward. As long as you continued pulling, he would be hard pressed to regain his feet.

The same applies to WWIINN™ conversations. Our hero validated Jenny, by saying, "I agree we wouldn't have argued if I had kept silent . . ." If he had disagreed with her the fight would have begun again. You can't argue with someone who agrees with you! After agreeing with Jenny our hero gently directed the conversation back on track.

How do you validate the other person? You simply say you understand, appreciate, respect or agree with whatever it is they have just said. To redirect the conversation, follow your validation with "and" or "and yet": then restate your observation or request. Resist all urges to say "but." "But" is the erasure word that negates everything that came before it. "I don't want to insult you, but . . ." means I'm about to knowingly insult you.

Consider eliminating the B-word from your vocabulary entirely. It triggers defensiveness and it weakens your effectiveness as a communicator.

There is something else we can learn from our two love-birds. In both scenarios our young lovers used a powerful tool. They did a great job of *describing* their observations and emotions instead of judging the other person or their intent.

Imagine how the conversation in Scenario 2 would have deteriorated if Jenny had said, "You make me so mad when you break your promises!" instead of stating her observations in the judgment-free manner she used when she described her interpretations and feelings.

Sometimes people refuse to change their behavior. This changes the game. When it becomes clear the other person is not interested in accommodating your request, it is time to establish consequences. Some people call them boundaries. Establishing consequences simply lets others know what will happen if they repeat the unacceptable behavior and what will happen if they choose the desired behavior.

Establishing consequences with a child might sound like this: "If you clean your room before 5:00 pm you can stay overnight with your friends. If your room is not clean by 5:00 pm you will not be allowed to go."

In a work situation it may sound like this: "If you continue to use that language in my presence, I will ask that you be removed from this work area."

In a personal relationship the following consequences may be appropriate. "If you continue to make fun of me when your friends come around, I will refuse to go out with you again." Or, "If you stop making fun of me in front of your friends, I will agree to see you again."

WWIINN™ conversations create alignment by increasing awareness, making requests and partnering in the solution. When you feel stress, they provide a powerful tool to restore your relationship. You may also find that the dialogue created in a WWIINN™ conversation expands your awareness! After all, sometimes we are the ones who may be interpreting the situation inaccurately.

Breakthrough Opportunity

Use the following worksheet to create your own WWIINN™ conversation.

Situation:

_____

_____

_____

W: What I really want is

_____

W: What I witnessed is

_____

_____

I: The impact of this is

_____

_____

I: What I think and feel is

_____

_____

N: What I need is

_____

_____

N: What do you need from me to be able to do that?

_____

_____

Chapter Eight
Lies, Damn Lies & Statistics

Now that we've identified the basic principles of Breakthrough living, I'd like to expose you to some of the lies that create so much pain in this world. See how many of them may be operating in your life.

1. If you loved me, you'd know what I want.

2. How you treat me is a reflection of my value and worth.

3. My current misery will pay you back for your past behavior.

4. People are basically good.

5. Life should be fair.

6. Life owes me, big time!

7. I don't have enough time.

8. I must always be right.

9. I should be farther along by now.

10. I shouldn't have to wait.

11. Don't sweat the small stuff.

12. People should be nice to me.

13. People should tell the truth.

14. I have to *(fill in any answer you can think of)*.

15. This shouldn't be happening.

16. Men are from Mars.

How did you do? If you think about it, you begin to see how pervasive these lies really are. I think that at one time or another I have believed all of them. In fact, they still trick me from time to time. So here's how to tell if you believe a lie: If you're in emotional pain, you've been seduced into believing a lie!

Perhaps you're thinking, "Hey wait a minute! Some of those things are not lies!" Let's take a closer look.

Lie: If you loved me, you'd know what I want.

Truth: No one is a mind reader. I may love you dearly and still have no clue what you want for dinner, let alone your birthday. Telling someone what you like or want or need does not suggest a problem with the relationship. Just the opposite is true. It means I feel comfortable sharing my desires with you. What you want is determined by your personal history and your current awareness. How could anyone truly know what that is? Besides, look at the pain you set yourself up for! If I guess wrong and don't know what you want, you've set it up to feel unloved! That's too high a price. Take a good dose of reality

and face the facts. You are lovable regard-
less of another's awareness of what you
want. Just ask for what you want. You'll
be much happier.

Lie: How you treat me is a reflection of my
value and worth (i.e. I made you do it).

Truth: How you treat me is a reflection of your
current awareness and unconscious
conversations! Your partner didn't cheat on
you because of you. They cheated because
of themselves. We do things for our own
reasons, not someone else's. We are solely
responsible for our thoughts, emotions and
actions. Our actions are the results of the
conversations we are living under at the
time we act. Can I say things designed to
hurt you? Of course. Can I be physically
abusive? Absolutely. Can I push your
buttons and invite you to operate under a
conversation that will cause you to react in
a predictable way? You know I can. Yet
each of us has a choice. The way I treat
you is a reflection of what's going on inside
of me. It's not your fault.

Lie: My current misery will pay you back for
your past behavior.

Truth: My current pain is of my own making.
Pain is a messenger. Once its message has
been delivered, we can send it on its way
any time we choose. Pain is a wound I

experience at my own hand. Even if you abused me horribly, I abuse myself again and again when I believe the lie that my martyrdom affects or punishes you in any way. Some people feel they will somehow be saying their abuse was O.K. if they release their pain. They believe their pain somehow protects them from getting hurt again. They think grief proves the depth of their love or their loss. Pain has a valid place in our lives. Fear and anger are powerful allies. Fear alerts us to danger, and our anger can generate the necessary adrenaline needed to fight off an enemy. That's good! When danger is real and present those emotions serve us well. When they prevent us from living, however, they are no longer useful. If we are experiencing ongoing pain after the actual event, we are choosing to experience it. I've heard it said that unforgiveness is like drinking poison and waiting for someone else to get sick.

Lie: People are basically good.

Truth: Some people are "good" and some are not. Some can be trusted and some can't. Be wise in selecting trustworthy friends.

Lie: Life should be fair.

Truth: Life *is* fair. Given the current conditions of everything, life is perfectly designed to be exactly what it is. When we say life should be fair, we are really saying that we think life should be different than it is. But it can't be. Fairness is a human construct that doesn't exist in nature. What is fair about a lion eating a gazelle? In the U.S. Constitution we are guaranteed life, liberty and the pursuit of happiness, but not fairness. Fairness/justice is half of a paradox, balanced against mercy/compassion. Some people subscribe to fairness as an ideal. Life makes no such promises. A great number of the people I've met whose favorite whine is "But that's not fair!" use a plea for fairness to excuse their own behavior or lack of action when they don't like the situation they're in.

Lie: Life owes me, big time!

Truth: While I think people are worthy of love and respect, I'm not sure we're entitled to anything. Entitlement is one small step from victim-hood. An entitlement mentality turns us into complainers and under-achievers while robbing us of the exquisite experience of gratitude. When I'm demonstrating love rather than demanding it, I am free to experience it. I've also observed that the people who receive respect or handouts or special treatment because they demanded it don't seem to enjoy it the way people who earn it do.

Lie: I don't have enough time.

Truth: We have all the time there is. By viewing time as the culprit we again become victims to our language. The truth is, time is our ally. We build a family, a reputation, a career and a life over time. The challenge is to construct our lives in such a way that time is not a constraint. In general, this means we need to focus on results, not on activity. We have to discipline ourselves to ask, "What do I *really* want?" and then be willing to pursue it, without concern for how long it takes. Life takes time.

Lie: I must always be right.

Truth: You're not. You can't be. When you humble yourself and admit there can be more than one right answer, you will feel the tension and fear melt right out of your body. You don't have to win every argument. You don't have to make others wrong. We all make mistakes. Our perceptions are not always accurate. You are not more lovable when you are right and you are not less lovable when you make an oops.

Lie: I should be farther along by now.

Truth: Your life has been perfectly designed to place you in your current situation. It is impossible to be any more successful than you are, given the choices you made in the past. You have created your life by your conversations, decisions and actions. If you desire a different outcome, change your circumstances by focusing on what you want, not what's wrong.

Lie: I shouldn't have to wait.

Truth: This sounds like entitlement again. The ability to delay gratification is the hallmark of maturity. Patience and perseverance will serve you much better than trying to win the lottery. The world is full of people who took 20 years to become an overnight success. Let time be your ally, not your enemy. Besides, whether we should or shouldn't have to wait doesn't change the reality that we are waiting. (Try that conversation next time you're stuck in traffic!)

Lie: Don't sweat the small stuff.

Truth: If it is triggering pain, it is significant. Ignoring the emotions just gives them more energy. Allow yourself to validate the significance of emotions. Once you have listened to the message your emotions are sending, they will usually leave on their own, gracefully. By the way, it is *not* all small stuff, either.

Lie: People should be nice to me.

Truth: I want people to be nice to me. I like it when people are nice to me. But if I *need* people to be nice to me I can expect a lot of pain because people will not always behave according to my definition of nice.

Given the current state of the world, this should not come as a surprise. Underneath the need for people to be nice is the lie that my value or worth is determined by someone's story about me. I've learned that what people think of me is none of my concern.

Lie: People should tell the truth.

Truth: People lie. People are exactly what they are. My desire for how I want them to be doesn't change reality. As a result, I may be careful to select relationships with people I can trust. I know some people who lie. I don't get all worked up about it. I am just very careful about believing what they tell me.

Lie: I have to (*fill in any answer you can think of*).

Truth: Everyone is always doing what he or she wants to do. You have free will and free choice (as free as it can be, given the way the brain filters our awareness). Even if you do something under duress, you have chosen to do it because you chose not to experience the consequences of not doing it. Stop telling people "I *have* to pick up my kids," or "I have to go to work." Start owning your choices and the consequences that come from them. Start saying, "I would prefer to stay home by myself tonight" instead of "I can't go out."

Replace "I have to" with "I'm going to" or
"I've decided to." It will change your life.

Lie: Men are from Mars.

Truth: I'm from Minnesota.

By noticing when you are in pain, you can take a
moment to determine if you've been seduced into believing a lie. Often just identifying the lie will bring clarity
and relief. Confusion is another signal that you are
struggling with a lie. When you feel confused, stop and
sort out the conversation you are hearing and the reality
you are sensing. Some people are expert crazy-makers.
When things aren't adding up and I'm starting to doubt
myself, it's a pretty good bet that someone is lying.

Another great way to eliminate pain and create pleasure
is to ask a question of yourself. Questions like these can
be very helpful when you want to feel differently:

1. How did I create this?

2. What am I holding on to that is creating this pain?

3. What do I appear to be afraid of?

4. How could I give love a chance?

5. How can I create a better game?

6. What do I really, *really* want?

7. What are the possibilities here?

8. Who do I love and how can I show it?

9. What excites me about my life, career, spouse
   or friends?

10. What can I do today to show I am 100% alive?

11. What risks am I prepared to take today?

12. How could this person be a solution and not a problem?

13. What am I pretending not to know?

Think of a situation you want to improve. Select 3 questions from above and answer the questions you've selected.

Situation to Improve:

Question 1:

_____

_____

_____

Question 2:

_____

_____

_____

Question 3:

_____

_____

_____

Questions like these create options. They'll highlight an unrealistic expectation, and they'll direct you towards an attitude of personal responsibility.

I had to use them myself last Father's Day.

On that Sunday, my daughter was vacationing out of state with friends, my son was working and my wife was scheduled to spend most of the day with two of her brothers. While I intellectually understood why I was likely to be alone all day I noticed I was feeling lonely and unloved. I didn't think it was fair!

I kept up my destructive silent conversations for a couple of hours. I even kept it up when I went outside and mowed the yard. Actually I "moped" the yard. "Woe is me," I said to myself as I slumped over the wheel and drove around and around in ever smaller circles.

After a while a new thought struggled to the front of my awareness. "I am responsible for how I'm feeling. How did I create this?" Once I allowed this thought to hit my brain I realized I hadn't done anything for my own father! So I called him up, (he lives in Florida) and proceeded to sing "Happy Father's Day To You" as loud as I could. When I stopped after two lines he immediately said "That's it?" To which I responded by finishing the song with all the power and volume I could muster. We both had a good laugh and a nice conversation. By the time we hung up I was feeling great.

With my newfound attitude I ran a couple of errands and called my son to see if he'd like a bite to eat after work. He was happy to get together and I overheard him tell a co-worker "I can't talk right now, my Dad is on the phone; we're *bonding*!" (He likes me, he really likes me!)

We ended up having a great meal and we laughed at all the challenges he was having as a stand-up comic. A few days later my daughter returned from vacation and called to get together. I had another great time with her and she gave me a picture of me holding her when she was just a few months old. Priceless!

Once again I was feeling loved and loving, and I was thrilled with the love my children were willing to share with me. I didn't feel entitled to their love, I felt honored by it. Now a new conversation slipped into my brain. "I have two of the greatest kids in the world!"

And I experienced the feelings of gratitude.

Isn't it fascinating that I was able to feel rejection when there was none? And yet had I allowed that feeling to continue I would not have called my father, and I probably would not have called my son. If I had continued to "awfulize" the situation, imagine how easily I could have turned off my son had he called me after work! If I'd been committed to being a victim, I'm sure I could have figured out a way to make him feel guilty for my loneliness. Then he could start to see me as a complaint and he'd have good reason to avoid me. I would have created rejection out of nothing!

My point is, even when people do ignore or reject me, how do I know I haven't set it up? By asking, "How did I create this?" I find a solution. By asking "Why do people reject me?" I just drive my lawn moper in ever-tightening circles.

Chapter Nine
Tools of the Trade

Over the last 14 years as a business consultant, I have worked with thousands of people from businesses of all sizes—from Fortune 25 companies to small ma and pa companies. One particular exercise routinely creates breakthrough more quickly and predictably than anything else.

Over the years I've refined it a half-dozen times to get it to work reliably. In the early days it occasionally wouldn't work with all personalities or all issues. While I reserve the right to improve upon it, I think that in its current form it will work for just about anyone.

The exercise is designed to uncover the cause of ongoing emotional pain or distress when that pain is no longer appropriate or healthy.

Some pain is completely appropriate. The sense of loss when a loved one dies is completely appropriate. And if that pain is felt and acknowledged and even embraced, it will help you become that much stronger. Sometimes, however, the pain doesn't recede, and people become debilitated by it.

When we are unable to recall a deceased person with a sense of love and gratitude and instead feel heartache and grief, we are believing a lie. When life presents an opportunity to stretch and grow, but we shrink from the opportunity with that "twisty" feeling in our guts, we are believing a lie. When we go to work dreading another day of office politics and power plays, we are believing a lie.

Let me share an example. Years ago I worked with a talented young man I'll call Chris. He was 30-something, with a new family and a promising career with a great company. I remember vividly how surprised our class was when he shared how anxious he was that he would soon fail and lose his job. By all outward appearances he was on a solid career path that he was more than able to follow successfully.

The whole room sat silent as he shared his fear that it was only a matter of time before he screwed up and lost everything. He was a fraud, and he was just waiting until everyone at work found out.

As I walked him through the exercise on the following pages, we quickly discovered the silent conversation that was creating the pervasive, nagging anxiety. He believed he was not smart enough to be successful, and he felt he did not deserve to be successful.

The origin of this thought was an incident he experienced right out of college. With enthusiasm and idealism at record levels, he and a college buddy decided to start a restaurant business after graduation. They felt their classmates would literally eat up a pizza parlor, so they raised $40,000 from friends and relatives and opened a pizza joint near their alma mater. In short order they lost the business and the forty grand.

The shame of failure and the guilt of losing his friend's and family's money left him devastated. His insides gnawed at him. "You idiot! How could you make such a stupid mistake! We trusted you and you let us down!" The accusations swirled just below his conscious thought and hadn't diminished in nearly 10 years.

Through the use of the worksheet he uncovered the lies that were eating him alive.

Lie #1: You should have known this would happen.

This is a variation of the perfection lie that all his choices should be right, i.e. he should be omniscient.

Lie #2: My current pain will pay back my investors.

This is a variation of the lie that my current pain is some type of compensation for past decisions. At some level Chris believed his pain was a sort of penance.

Lie #3: Because I failed, I am a failure.

Chris had come to let his failure become his identity, rather than just an event.

As he worked through the exercise, Chris saw the truth. Failure could never define him; it was his *response* to failure that would ultimately determine his character.

At one point in the exercise I asked him to imagine that this truth were written inside his head as a sort of filter. I asked him what his life would be like if every time he looked out his eyeballs he saw everything through this newly discovered truth.

He closed his eyes and thought for a moment. "I would-n't be afraid to speak or make decisions," he replied. "I would look forward to challenges, and my wife would be thrilled."

Then I asked him to mentally imagine a situation that would typically trigger those lies and I asked him to imagine the truth immediately replacing the lie.

He started to smile.

I asked him what was happening. He said, "I'm a reli-gious person and I've prayed over this for years. But every time I gave the problem to the Lord, I would take it back when I was done praying. When I closed my eyes just now I saw the whole pizza restaurant burst into flames and burn to the ground. When I looked into the rubble I found a golden brick, which represented the truth that only my response to failure mattered. And in my mind's eye I picked up that brick and slipped it into the foundation of my mansion in heaven."

We were speechless.

Over the next six weeks of class I checked in with Chris. "I'm doing great!" he said. "If I ever get that little twinge I just remember the truth and it goes away."

After Chris finished the leadership program, I lost touch with him for a couple of years. We met again when he invited me to his company to see if I could help with a project he was leading. Of course, I was dying to know if he was still free from those lies. He smiled broadly. "They've never come back."

People only believe lies out of ignorance. We mistakenly believe them to be true. When we examine a thought carefully and find it to be untrue, it is remarkably easy to replace it with the truth.

I encourage you to actually work through the following exercise rather than simply read it. To do it justice you'll need anywhere from 20 to 40 minutes to complete it. You may even want to have a trusted friend read the instructions and help you talk through the thoughts and emotions that surface. If at any point your emotions threaten to overwhelm you, simply pause and breathe deeply to relieve the tension in your body.

Since this will be your first experience with this exercise, please select an issue that is relatively benign. This will help you learn the process. Once you become familiar with how the process works you can tackle larger issues with confidence.

The instructions for filling in the worksheet follow the worksheet on page 116.

Breakthrough Worksheet

Instructions:

Select a situation that upsets you or limits your success. If this is your first experience with this exercise, select an issue that is only mildly or moderately painful. Once you master the process you may use it to resolve more significant issues.

1. The situation that appears to upset me is:

   _____

   _____

   _____

2. The belief that is limiting me in this situation is:

   _____

   _____

   _____

3. This belief has been present since_____, and has cost me:

   _____

   _____

   _____

4. I now realize my pain is caused by believing a lie. I have been believing the lie that:

   _____

   _____

   _____

5. The truth is:

_____

_____

6. As I think about this truth I feel:

_____

_____

7. I can see that understanding this difference will bring me the following benefits:

_____

_____

_____

8. To practice living in accordance with this insight, I commit to the following action before midnight tonight:

_____

_____

9. I also commit to

_____

within the next week.

10. The next time I encounter a situation like this I have several options:

I can_____

I can_____

or I may choose to _____

Instructions for the Breakthrough Worksheet

1. Fill in a brief description of what is causing you pain. Perhaps you are feeling frustrated because you are not getting the advancement you desire in your career. Perhaps someone cheated or mistreated you. Perhaps a friend or family member is doing something that offends or hurts. Write down the situation you face that *appears* to be creating your discomfort and then take a deep, cleansing breath. Breathe in through your nose and out through your mouth. Allow yourself to relax as you breathe the stress right out of your body. If at any time during the exercise you notice yourself feeling stress, consciously stop for a moment and *breathe*.

2. Identify the belief that is causing pain. Your limiting belief will often take the form of "I can't succeed because_____" or "people should/shouldn't_____." For example, If I've been lied to I may think that "People should keep their promises." Perhaps I feel frustrated because I believe someone "won't let me succeed" or "I don't have the necessary abilities to succeed." Remember to breathe any time you feel yourself getting anxious or uncomfortable.

3. On line 3 put in the date you first noticed this belief was operating in your life. Did it originate in second grade because of a significant emotional event? Have you always believed it? Then identify what keeping this belief has cost you in terms of success, happiness, and relationships.

4. On line 4 you will need to go a bit deeper. Your pain comes from the clash between how you believe the world should be and how it actually is. Somewhere in your answer to line 2 is a lie. Using the example that "People should keep their promises" we could ask the question "Why?" And we may get the answer, "Because honesty and integrity are good." To which we might respond, "Are all people good?" This question might help us realize that some people are basically honest and some people are not. The lie is that we *need* people to be honest or that we *need* them to have our values. Going deeper still, it may become clear that the lie we are believing is that if people do not keep their promises, it suggests that we are somehow not worthy of their respect. Perhaps we have been duped into believing that the way people treat us reflects our basic value and worth as a human being! Take the time to identify the deepest lie you can; the lie that is actually causing this pain. (Keep in mind that the most common lies are that we believe we *need* something to be a certain way instead of realizing we simply *want* it to be a certain way or that we are invalid and unworthy unless we get a certain response from people or life.)

5. On line 5, please identify the truth. You may wish to try writing it several times on a piece of scratch paper until you get the wording just right. To help make your statement even more powerful, write out your truth in the first person,

present tense. For example you may write "While I prefer honesty in all my relationships, I do not need people to live by my values to be happy." Or maybe "I do not need to be right to prove I am competent and lovable. I am lovable even when I make a mistake." A powerful technique is to turn the lie around. If the thought that is vexing you is, "He should respect me." Turn it around to "I need to respect him," or "I need to respect myself." Then the truth of how you could respond will often become brilliantly clear.

6. Notice the emotions this new thought creates. If any anxiety persists, identify the lie beneath it and work the exercise on that.

7. On line 7 imagine how you would benefit from this more accurate way of viewing the world. Imagine how your relationships, family or career would be affected if you lived this way consistently. Take a moment to record the benefits. For example, without this lie I would feel peaceful, happy, sane and calm. I would make certain changes, etc.

8. Now it is time for action. On line 8, please make a commitment to act in accordance with your new awareness. Perhaps it is a simple act of consciously saying "I now release and cancel my need for other people to live according to my values." You may wish to formalize your new insight by writing your lie on a piece of paper and ceremoniously burning it. Perhaps you will choose to watch the sunset tonight and as it sets you will say to yourself "I release my need to always be right, and I know the sun will rise tomorrow even if I make a

mistake today." Perhaps you will commit to talk with a friend about this exercise (maybe even the person who helped you see you had been living under a false belief!)

9. On line 9 you are asked to take another action to prove to yourself you are acting under your new belief system. Look at your calendar and schedule an action you know will cement this new reality in your mind. (Perhaps a celebration of some kind?)

10. On line 10, please imagine how you could respond when you encounter this type of situation in the future. List at least three different responses that would allow you to confidently manage the situation. If need be, you can always fill out another worksheet if you realize more than one lie was embedded in your situation.[1,2]

---

1 The Breakthrough Worksheet was designed to help people live happier, more successful lives by challenging the lies that have crept into their belief systems. It is not a replacement for therapy or counseling. To receive more information about our Breakthrough products and workshops for yourself or your business please call 763-477-5599 or write to us at Mills and Associates, Inc., 6810 Greenfield Road, Loretto, MN. 55357. If you wish, you may email your requests and comments to *wmillsa@mindspring.com*. William Mills and Associates, Inc. is a consulting organization dedicated to helping its clients achieve breakthrough results. We specialize in Strategic Planning and Implementation, Optimizing Your Workplace, and Breakthrough Relationships. We support all our work with a 100% money-back guarantee.

2 The Breakthrough Worksheet is a merging and evolution of ideas incorporated from Dr. Michael Ryce, Anthony Robbins, Neurolinguistic Programming and the writings of L.S. Barksdale. To receive a copy of the worksheet visit our website at: *www.thebreakthroughbook.com*

Chapter Ten
Creating Breakthrough

"Whatever you can do, or dream you can, begin it. Boldness has genius, power and magic in it."

—Goethe

To really experience breakthrough requires an inner victory first. We are bombarded with stimuli and people and events that entice us to believe the battle is "out there." We have a wealth of hopes, dreams and goals for the life we want to live, and when we see the problems and roadblocks standing between our future and today, we interpret them as reality. They become the constraints that limit what is possible.

My friend Terry Miller says that when you set a goal to lose weight, the first thing that shows up is banana cream pie. I think Terry is half right. What actually shows up is Ben & Jerry's Cherry Garcia ice cream.

The point is, Cherry Garcia, poor employee morale, inflexible policies, a down economy or all the other constraints that stop us in our tracks only exist by agreement. If we think a constraint "out there" is real, it may as well be. But what if its existence is not actually a constraint?

What if you believed that the economy was depressed *and* you were still going to grow your company? What if you only had 24 hours a day and you were still going to honor your faith, your family, your career and yourself?

How is it that certain people are able to create mind-boggling results when so many of us struggle just to get to daycare before they close?

How does a Bill Gates drop out of college to become the nation's richest man? How does a Mother Theresa, who has taken a vow of poverty, become a world leader synonymous with love and compassion while attracting millions of dollars to her efforts all around the world?

I would like to offer the possibility that the people who achieve results at these huge orders of magnitude are operating under a different reality. They see things we don't see.

These people are not defying the laws of gravity and physics. They have opened themselves to a world where the solutions are "out there" and the battle lies within.

Breakthrough people operate under a different reality, a reality shaped in general by their conversations and specifically by their commitments and their complaints. When you dissect a complaint, what do you find? You find a person at odds with reality, a person with an inaccurate view of the world. (I can hear your grumbling beginning already. "I can't believe what this guy is saying!" "That's not true! My complaints are valid!")

A complaint accompanies emotional discomfort. We are angry, frustrated, hurt or fearful when we complain. In the act of complaining we are resisting the existence of the thing we are complaining about. Not only does the complainer focus on what's wrong, they focus on the degree of wrongness.

Complainer 1: I can't believe Jody did this to me. It's terrible! She is so inconsiderate!

Complainer 2: I have a terrible manager. He doesn't know the first thing about what we do. He is so stupid.

In Complainer 1's reality, Jody is a constraint to her happiness and peace of mind. Complainer 2's reality is constrained by a stupid boss. There is not a lot of opportunity in a reality constrained by insensitive and stupid people. The more you resist the facts that such people and their behaviors exist and that you can not control them, you will be in pain. You will also be constrained because you'll focus on the wrong things.

The first step to creating a reality of possibility is to accept the existence of an unwanted reality. I know this can be a bit confusing at first, so let me use the following example as an illustration.

Your 13-year-old child never cleans his room and he rarely does his household chores without lots of reminders and nagging. This is an unwanted reality in your life. When you complain about the mess and undone chores, you feel stress, frustration and anger. In your child's world you have become the complaint. You have become the stressed-out, angry and frustrated parent who is powerless over a 13-year-old.

Notice that your complaining doesn't remove the unwanted reality. The mess remains. As you resist the existence of the mess you are reinforcing your belief that "this should not be," all the while the mess is not moved. Then your focus shifts to "you should obey me," even though you know that obedience is voluntary. Your brain is struggling with the paradox. The mess should not be and yet it is. You should obey me, yet you don't. The frustration escalates right along with your growing awareness that you are powerless. You do not control the universe.

Your complaint has now shaped your reality. You have become an angry, helpless victim.

Earlier we discussed TUA, total unconditional acceptance. This is a deeper inspection of that idea. What if you trained yourself to think, "This mess is an unwanted reality. I accept that it exists. I am now searching for the best response."

Or, try this one. "My boss does things that differ from my point of view. This is an unwanted reality. I am now looking for a response that will help us both be happy." The more we complain about something, the more solid and immovable it becomes in our reality. The complaint that "You can't fight city hall!" prevents thousands from trying.

List your most common complaints and notice the reality they create:

Complaint	Created Reality
Example: I hate lazy, stupid people.	My emotions and life are at risk every time I interact with "those" people.

I had a chance to practice my own advice this past summer. I was helping my wife put 300 bales of hay in our barn. Every ten minutes or so, I had to stop because my lungs were burning and aching. I thought I was out of shape or that I had some sort of bronchial infection.

A few days later my doctor suggested I was suffering from acid reflux and prescribed a strong antacid. We also agreed that I would undergo a stress test just to be sure there was nothing wrong with my heart. The day of my stress test was a Friday that coincided with my 5th wedding anniversary with Lisa. I drove myself to the hospital, got hooked up to the monitor and started walking on the treadmill. Sure enough my lungs started to burn. The technician stopped the test and called for a cardiologist.

They immediately ordered an angiogram, injecting dye into my arteries to check for blockages. Again, they stopped the test abruptly and called for the cardiologist. He looked at the monitors for a few seconds, put his hand on my shoulder and said, "You're not going anywhere, bud. First thing Monday morning we need to perform triple bypass surgery." Then he left the room.

Talk about unwanted realities! I'm only 45! I'm too young for this! This shouldn't be happening to me! It's not fair! My chest started to ache and I became short of breath. Thankfully, I realized I was resisting reality, and my resistance was creating a physical consequence!

I caught myself and said to the nurse, "This is really happening, isn't it?" She said, "Yes, it is." Then I asked "What do we need to do to have a happy ending?"

The moment I said "This is really happening" my stress disappeared. I was calm and coolheaded as we planned my therapy. Not only was I calm in that moment, my fear never returned. They put me on bed rest and oxygen and made me lie still over the weekend until they could operate.

I thought everyone was being overly dramatic until I learned that I had blockages in all three major coronary arteries. One contained a 100% blockage, another was 90% blocked and the third, on the back side of my heart, was 75% blocked. They weren't sure why I was even able to walk!

As a result of that experience I have been re-doubling my efforts to accept the existence of unwanted realities in my life. Every time I do, they have ceased to be constraints and I find myself peacefully moving beyond them.

I've noticed something else as well. When I eliminate resistance, peace and joy move in to fill the void. It's as if resistance blocks my sense of my place in the world, and the practice of acceptance allows me to locate myself, which brings a sense of well-being. When I'm resisting reality I'm setting myself in judgment over the world. From that position I am under the illusion I can control things that I really have no control over at all. When I accept an unwanted reality I am flowing with life, not against it.

I now suspect that joy, peace and love are the natural programmed state of the human being. We override that programming when we resist the unwanted realities in ourselves and in our lives. I don't think peace actually fills the void when we eliminate judgment and resistance. I think it is always there, patiently waiting for us to tire of railing against the injustices and problems that are simply a natural part of life. When we complain about the world as it is, we lose our peace.

Now let's turn our attention to a major component of breakthrough; our commitments.

I've heard it said that a commitment is a promise you make that you will not break. There is magic in commitment. Most of us fail to make promises. Instead we make predictions. We set goals, we make New Year's resolutions. You can almost hear Failure laughing in the shadows as the division managers squirm to answer the question, "What will we accomplish this year?"

"Well, our GOAL is to grow 15%," they say, "but you know, with the economy the way it is I'd be happy just staying even."

"Last year we grew 3%, so we feel we can do 4% this year. After all that's a 33% improvement!" they say, hoping no one challenges their logic.

It's all goals and prediction and it leaves people flat.

Breakthrough is not about predictions based upon extrapolations. To achieve breakthrough you need to get to a place of not knowing. Knowing is the enemy because it is predicated on the past. Knowing pressures us to follow the beaten path, to think the same thoughts and get the same results. Knowing precludes real thinking and blocks possibilities from getting through our filters.

Not knowing is alive with possibility and inventions.

Q: How will you get her to notice you?

A: I don't know, I just will.

Q: How will you ever get your project done in time?

A: I don't know, I'll have to get creative and do whatever it takes.

Q: How will you reduce your costs while improving your service?

A: I don't know, we'll just keep working it until we succeed.

Two men have influenced me greatly on this subject: David McNally and Terry Miller.[1] David posed a question to me that I have in turn posed to thousands of people. In fact, I often end my workshops with it and the answer is always the same.

I'll ask a room full of people to think of the times when they were 100% committed to achieving specific results in their lives. I ask them to think of those times when they absolutely knew they would be successful because they had *decided* to be. They were dialed in and locked on. There was no possibility of failure because they

---

1 David McNally is the author of *Even Eagles Need a Push*. Terry Miller is a business consultant and mentor.

simply wouldn't allow it. Now I'd like you to do the same. Please take a moment to recall those times when you have been completely committed to achieving a specific outcome, and begin reading again when you have them in mind.

Notice the number of times you can recall being totally committed are relatively few. Now please answer this question: When you have fully committed yourself to achieving a specific goal or outcome, what percentage of the time did you actually achieve it?

Write your answer here:

When fully committed I have been successful ____% of the time.

When I ask this question of a group of people, I ask them to raise their hand if their answer is 80% or above. What do you think happens? Nearly every hand goes up. When I ask people to keep their hand raised if their answer is 90% or above, only a few hands will drop away. Then I ask people to keep their hands up if their answer was 100%, and again most hands stay up. Depending on the group, anywhere from two thirds to as many as 100% of the people polled have never experienced failure when they have fully committed themselves to achieving something.

Consider the implications of this discovery. Perhaps we don't have cash flow problems, quality problems, vendor or technology problems. Perhaps we don't have problems with our families, friends and co-workers. Maybe we have commitment problems.

Perhaps we are interested in so many things, we have forgotten what we are committed to. When was the last time your sales force *promised* the number of sales they would make? When did you last review your life and establish the four or five commitments that would define your purpose and legacy?

Commitments are powerful because the most committed person ultimately wins. When complainers are more committed to their point of view than others are to a positive result, a team, department or marriage is doomed.

When people dedicate themselves to creating a great life, a great marriage or a great company, it generally succeeds.

When the founders of the United States of America transformed their interest in living in a free country into a commitment to create one, they put their commitment into a Declaration of Independence. When JFK declared that we would put a man on the moon before the next decade, it happened. A declaration is part of commitment. Whether public or private at first, it soon becomes public when you act on it.

As a senior in high school I learned that the fall play was to be *The Music Man*. I immediately decided that I would win the leading role, and I committed myself to making it happen. Obstacles immediately appeared. The role required singing solos and dancing. I had never done either in front of someone else, aside from singing with a large group of classmates. The director, Ms. Nelson (who never selected a play without a couple of people in mind) already knew who she wanted in the lead roles. I was not one of those people. In fact, though I'd been in plays before, I'd never had a lead part. And finally, tryouts were only a few days away and we were not allowed to see the script before hand. We would be given parts to read cold at the audition. But I was committed. I went to music store after music store until I found the Music Man sound track on a vinyl record (this was 1974). The play's most memorable song is probably "Trouble in River City," which is a syncopated song sung to a fast, bouncing rhythm. I figured it would be used at the singing tryouts.

Putting the record on my dad's turntable I played the song over and over. I tried to sing along but I couldn't keep up—it was too many words and they came too fast. Try as I might, I couldn't follow along for more than a few seconds. But I kept playing it over and over and over.

I wore that record out playing that song till I had to go to bed. And I was not making progress. The next morning I picked out the uniform that helped me feel the most comfortable—a blue chambray shirt and my jeans with all the patches and the ripped-out knee. Throughout the day I tried to remember the words to the song, but I could only get the first sentence to flow before I became tongue-tied by the rhythm and speed.

And all too soon it was tryouts. When it was time for the singing audition Collin, Gordon, Rob and I all raised our hands and stepped forward. Collin and Gordon were the clear favorites. Tall and strong compared to all 130 pounds of me, they looked like leading men. I looked like their little brother. But I was switched on!

They lined the four of us up and gave us the words to "Trouble in River City." They asked us to all sing together. The director told Peter, our local piano virtuoso to begin and he dove into the music with gusto.

We each found our note, took a deep breath and began to sing, but the music moved so fast you couldn't read the words.

With the page blurring in front of me I kept willing myself through the lyrics until it dawned on me that Gordon, Collin and Rob had stopped singing. I didn't need to read the words anymore; they were coming out of me on automatic pilot.

When I finally stopped, the room went silent. The play director and the choir director were frowning and whispering. "You are a tenor," said the choir director. "This part requires a tenor. Why haven't you ever been in choir?"

"I don't know."

"Well, you've certainly made this difficult for me," said Ms. Nelson.

A few days later I was awarded the lead. I have used that experience over and over again to push myself into situations that scared me to death.

Now fast forward to the summer of 2000. I had created a coaching workshop to teach managers and leaders how to have conversations with employees and teammates that would help them re-align with the vision and values of their organization. We named the workshop *Coaching with Confidence*, and we started searching for consultants to distribute it across the country. Terry Miller acted as my personal coach and he asked me what I was willing to commit to achieving. His eyes must have rolled back in his head when I told him I wanted 10 more distributors by year end, 50 distributors in 2001 and 100 by the end of 2002.

"Bill," he said, "Get out of your head. Stop predicting."

"What do you mean?"

"I didn't ask for your prediction about the future, I asked what future are you committed to creating. So, again, what number of distributors do you want before year end, a number that you don't know how to get to."

"Well," I said, "I don't know how to get to 100."
"Great!" he replied. "What are you feeling?"

"I'm scared. My plate is full. I have these consulting projects that are taking all my time. I don't know where to find the time to get this all done." (Notice how subtle and reasonable my complaint sounded? Poor Bill, he doesn't have the time to reach his goals!)

Then Terry brought out the big guns. "That's simple, Bill. Just create a solution that is not constrained by time or effort."

If he hadn't been 1200 miles away I would have slapped him. "It's not nice to tease people," I thought. Then I said, "Well, if time and effort are not constraints, then maybe I should get all this done and take every Friday off as well."

"Now you've got it!" Terry exclaimed. I wanted to bang my head with the telephone. Terry Miller must not understand sarcasm.

But then that queasy feeling in my gut turned into the same determination I experienced in high school and I made the commitment. Nothing happened for the next two months. It was nearly October and we were 80 distributors short of what I had promised. Terry told me I should schedule my breakthrough in October. (Terry really does live in a different reality, doesn't he? Whoever heard of scheduling a breakthrough?)

So I "scheduled" my breakthrough for October. I looked at my calendar and saw I had only one opportunity. Lisa and I had a booth at a Society of Human Resource Managers (SHRM) conference. Maybe we could convince eighty HR managers to become distributors inside their company. Ha!

Our doubts are traitors and make us lose the good we oft might win by fearing to attempt.
—Shakespeare

When you get right down to the root of the meaning of the word "succeed," you find it simply means to follow through.

The day of the conference came. Our booth was off the beaten path in a hall with about sixty other vendors. The SHRM members had no occasion to enter the hall except for lunch because all their workshops were held in another part of the building. And their lunch hour was so short they had barely enough time to eat and run back to their next sessions.

The words to *Trouble in River City* started bouncing through my head.

If Mohammed wasn't coming to the mountain I would bring the mountain to Mohammed. I was committed! I grabbed a handful of brochures and started hunting. I would approach a lunch table full of HR managers and offer them a brochure. As people turned to see what I was doing, I would offer a brochure and ask "Would you like one, too?" and nod my head yes. Everyone took one. Then I would give them a quick explanation of our process and invite them to our booth.

I got ZIP. Nothing came of it. They ate their lunches and threw $100 worth of my brochures in the trash on their way out.

Then I narrowed my eyes and turned my attention on the sixty vendors in the now nearly empty hall.

One of the other booths was manned by someone I had briefly met about eight years earlier. As we got re-acquainted he showed an interest in our workshop. It turns out he had developed a network of consultants who purchased his assessment products, and he wanted to expand into my type of workshops and materials.

"How many distributors do you have?" I asked.

"Oh, I think we have about 85," he replied.

See Bill. See Bill smile.

We signed the papers later in December, just days short of the date I had committed to.

My newest commitment is for Lisa and me to retire by 2007 with a passive income in excess of $200,000 a year. I'm going to do it by teaching other consultants and executives how to earn a six-figure income while working two weeks a month using a consulting model I'm currently using.[3]

Breakthrough living requires breakthrough thinking. The real battle lies within; the solutions are all out there.

The greatest key to breakthrough is to create a reality free from the constraints of time, effort and money. This reality is created by your conversations and their correlating actions.

As I was reflecting on the nature of breakthrough it became clear that there are only 4 activities in life.[4] By reorganizing yourself in these four activities, you greatly enhance your chances of breakthrough.

Activity 1: Administrative Activities

Administrative activities refer to those things that need to be done (paying bills, cleaning your house, filling out paperwork, etc. etc.). These things do not create breakthrough, they eat up your time.

Breakthrough Strategy

Eliminate, delegate or simplify administrative duties. If it feels like a duty and your heart is not in it, find a way to shrink its impact on your life. Free up as much time as you possibly can for living.

---

3 For more information on this opportunity visit *www.executivegroupinc.net*.
4 These concepts were inspired by the late William McGrane. He felt people should play 100 days, prepare 100 days, and work 100 days each year.

Activity 2: Advancing Activities

Advancing activities are the high-payoff activities that advance you toward your commitments. They are often uncomfortable, yet necessary. They are only uncomfortable if we resist them. They are much easier to handle with time and with the knowledge that they are the price of success. Advancing activities directly produce achievement and progress. Activities that build relationships, make sales, get the right things done; these are advancing activities (and there aren't all that many of them). One of the best things about advancing activities is that they generate enthusiasm and energy. People who feel burned out have either stopped working on advancing activities or they have not selected a life goal worth committing to.

Breakthrough Strategy

Schedule big blocks of time for advancing activities. Half days or full days work best. Do whatever it takes to limit distractions and work in at least 90 minute segments. Take a five minute mental break every twenty to thirty minutes, but don't take phone calls or allow interruptions. Don't change your focus. I do a tremendous amount of creative work in restaurants because the environment works perfectly for me. Find a place that allows you to do your best. If your highest pay activities require you to work with other people ask them to help you make that time effective and productive.

Activity 3: Rejuvenating Activities

Rejuvenating activities give you the energy you need for activities 2 and 4. Vacations, hobbies, alone time, social time, exercise, spiritual pursuits, or any activity that brings acceptance, compassion or peace is a rejuvenating activity. You need lots of these activities. I currently work a four-day week and I'm on track to a 10-day month. It is the ideas that come to me and energy I receive during my rejuvenating activities that make it possible.

Breakthrough Strategy

Spend the time to learn which activities truly feed your soul. Experiment with activities that take only a few minutes up to several days to do properly. Then when you have a free afternoon you can select from a list of quick activities and when you have more time you can work off a larger list. Make sure your list includes things you can do at home as well as away from home. Work with your life partner to include his or her favorite activities as well. Many of your rejuvenating activities can be spontaneous but I find that looking forward to a planned activity is very satisfying as well. Lisa and I try to schedule vacations out as far as one or two years in advance.

Activity 4: Breakthrough Activity

This category is the least understood and most overlooked. It is also the most important. When teamed with rejuvenating activities, it is deeply energizing. Two breakthrough activities are making commitments and declarations. Other breakthrough activities are creating annuity and passive results. Thinking up ways to create leverage is a breakthrough activity. Questions to ask yourself might include: How can I build a solution that can be replicated 1000 times? How can I teach 50 or 500 or 5000 people at once? How can I make my sales presentations to 100 buyers one time rather than one buyer a hundred times? How can I use a mortgage or loan to purchase an asset instead of my own money? What can I create, write, paint or record that can produce royalties every time it is sold? What relationships can I create that will reward people for rewarding me? How could I change the game in such a way that I am 10 times happier or 100 times more fulfilled?

Breakthrough is primarily a thinking activity, and it is even stronger when shared with a friend. Set aside time for brainstorming as a family, team or department. Ask yourselves: "What system can we create to simplify, automate, prevent or eliminate the tasks no one enjoys?" "What could we do to get to a completely new level of love and romance?" or "What activities can we combine to enhance our results and save time?" (For example if you and your mate decide you want to spend more time together, exercise and eat healthy, could you power-walk together at the warehouse food store as you carry baskets instead of push carts and together select the most healthy items?)

Breakthrough Strategy

> Schedule your breakthrough. Dedicate time on your calendar to setting new standards of success for yourself. Use that time to ask lots of questions like, "What if . . .?" and "How could I . . .?" The quality of the question will be a huge determinant of your breakthrough.

Breakthrough living begins with breakthrough thinking. Don't worry about the ideas that fall a bit short. Each one serves its purpose of coaxing you into a reality of abundance, possibility and solutions.

One of my clients is a large furniture retailer in the Minneapolis/St. Paul area. The company has several locations, over 800 employees and it is doubling in size every three to four years.

One of the client's departments is responsible for the site maintenance of all the locations. During a possibility exercise, the team identified a major frustration. Any manager or supervisor at any location could call any maintenance team member and request service. This was done to ensure that every store was always looking its best. The unintended consequence of all this empowerment was immediate. Five or six managers would notice a maintenance issue and leave a voice mail or e-mail request with up to five different team members, who would all swing into action. This system created tremendous duplication of effort, not to mention the frustration caused when a team member would arrive to solve a problem only to find it had been resolved earlier that day.

As the team members considered how to resolve the issue, they hit on the idea of an electronic in-board. By utilizing their existing e-mail system, teammates could give real-time status reports to each other and all managers and supervisors at a site needing attention. The first person to hear of a problem would schedule the repair and notify all appropriate parties with a few keystrokes. The solution prevented multiple requests and duplication of efforts. Their most conservative estimates indicate they have saved over 500 man-hours with this simple solution. In hindsight, it's simple. But it only became simple when the team shifted their awareness to include possibility.

Amazing things happen when people take the time to stop working *in* their businesses and relationships and they start working on the *design* of their businesses and relationships. Breakthrough activities are design activities.

Breakthrough Opportunity

How can I design my relationships to create more happiness? How can I design my work to be more rewarding and require less time?

Current frustration or constraint

_____

_____

Preferred future state/outcome

_____

_____

_____

Breakthrough ideas

_____

_____

_____

My commitment

_____

_____

We started this chapter with an exploration of how complaints and commitments shape our reality and thereby shape what is possible. We end on the need to spend time mentally exploring possibility.

One of my clients recently said to me, "So you're telling me it's just a mind game?" I assured him that it has always been a mind game. The difference is that these approaches make it a game you can win because it's your game. When society, bosses, co-workers and past experiences tell us what is possible, we buy into somebody else's game. The starting point of this new game is the quality of your conversations. When you see the effects our conversations have on our lives you start to see there is no such thing as an idle conversation. Conversations are actions that produce specific results!

Breakthrough conversations with yourself and others will have a cumulative effect on your life. Before you know it, you'll be more at ease and more productive. Problems and constraints will melt away, leaving in their place possibility and abundance. Then one day you'll look around and say, "I've passed through the looking glass. I'm on the other side of complexity."

You will have experienced Breakthrough.

Epilogue

If you have benefited from this book please let us know! If you've experienced breakthrough in your life please tell us. We love success stories!

If you would permit your breakthrough story to be used in future books or publications, please send us your story and include a statement allowing us to use your story accordingly. We are currently gathering material for Breakthrough approaches to Career Success, Parenting, Weight Loss & Health, Spiritual Growth, and Marriage.

Success stories can be mailed to:

William Mills and Associates, Inc.
Success Story Editor
6810 Greenfield Rd.
Loretto, MN 55357

If you would like Bill to be a keynote speaker, or to host a workshop, or if you would like information about our Breakthrough Retreats and other services, please contact us at 1-800-853-5545, or email us at:

wmillsa@mindspring.com
Our website address is: **thebreakthroughbook.com**

Thank you.

P.S. We can also accommodate discount pricing for large orders of *Breakthrough!*